I AM THIRD

KINITA SCHRIPSEMA

I AM THIRD

REDEEMING THE PATH

A JOURNEY THROUGH PARENTING AND ADOPTION

credo
house publishers

Published in the United States of America by Credo House Publishers,
a division of Credo Communications LLC, Grand Rapids, Michigan
credohousepublishers.com

ISBN: 978-1-62586-225-9

Cover by Swapnil Shinde
Interior by Believe Book Design
Editing by Donna Huisjen

First edition

Contents

Preface

A message from Ken

Looking in the rearview mirror is always a good opportunity to reflect on where we've been and what brought us to where we are today. This book is a look in the rearview mirror and an opportunity to share with you, the reader, what has been learned from hard work, successes, and failures.

As with any marriage, when Kinita came into my life we had no idea what we were getting ourselves into. She was the first Indian (from India) I had ever met. I had never talked to a person from India, much less dated or married one. I knew nothing of the Indian culture. As I think back, growing up as a Dutch American in a heavily populated Dutch-immigrant city, I had no way to articulate what my culture was, either.

There wasn't much interest in my family in international travel or cultural education. We were patriotic Americans who didn't spend much time evaluating our culture or comparing it to other cultures. I guess I could say that lacking an interest in other cultures was part of our culture.

Our marriage was built on many core values we both agreed with. We had similar passions, a similar faith experience, and similar dreams for what our family would look like. Two years into our marriage, our first son arrived. By his third birthday, we were in the full swing of many challenges. We found ourselves parenting a strong-willed child who cut his teeth on dividing and conquering, pushing us to a whole new level of conversation.

We look back now and say that we didn't struggle with racial differences, but we did learn that our personalities and our different cultures contributed significantly to our parenting challenges. We sought help and walked through difficult and turbulent times with the help of counselors and mentors.

While we came from extremely different family backgrounds, we learned about what we both brought into the marriage from our own families of origin; this included some helpful and some not-so-helpful traits. We learned much about our own personalities, strengths, and weaknesses and how all of them contributed to our present family dynamics.

This Indian woman I married was gifted in ways I had never encountered before. She was strong, decisive, and passionate. She loved boundaries; clear communication; resolving conflict; and, in parenting, clearly conveyed that a strong-willed child should never win the battle of the wills. I, on the other hand, was more tender, nurturing, compassionate—as our therapist described it, I was a man with porous boundaries who was "easy and natural." In all honesty, I was a pushover.

While I tended to accommodate and avoid conflict, Kinita was wired for holding boundaries and seeking unity, truth, and reconciliation. She wanted us to be on the same page. She wanted us to operate as a team. She wanted to empower and equip our children and to help them become "the best version of their true selves"—one of her favorite phrases.

As I look back at those years of child-rearing, I recognize with amazement how much we have grown. It took a lot of hard work to identify and eradicate our own "junk" while we rose to the task of raising four children. In so many ways, we can say today that parenting made us better people. We didn't always get it right, but we kept at it and kept learning through the failures and the successes. It also took *both* of us, with our very different perspectives and gifts. I can confidently say today that Kinita made me a better husband and father.

While we believe that God is intimately involved in the shaping and forming of each one of us, I can also confidently say that Kinita was instrumental in the shaping, empowering, and equipping of our children in ways in which I wasn't gifted.

This book is a result of those many years of hard work. She has much to offer any parent or couple in the throes of parenting. I am thankful you picked up this book. You won't be sorry you did.

May God bless you on your own journey of parenting!

Introduction

Where it all began

The idea of caring about adoptions was planted in me in high school when I ran a mini marathon to help raise money for the Children's Adoption Program in Ontario, Canada. Little did I know then how my life would be forever changed by adoption. After college, I would marry the man of my dreams and have three handsome sons with him. Our family was complete, or so we thought, . . . until our daughter joined us.

On more than one occasion I had been told by others that we must have adopted "because we wanted more children" or "because we weren't satisfied with just boys" or "because we had a desperate need for a girl." For me, all of these were false statements. The truth was that we weren't looking to adopt out of some unmet need. Here is some unsolicited advice. When you know someone—a friend or family member—who is considering foster care or adoption, learn to *ask* them to share their "why" rather than *telling* them why they chose their journey of either foster care or adoption. And don't *question* their choice to foster or adopt; ask questions to learn and find ways to support them in their journey. . . . They will need it.

With three growing sons, our house and schedules were quite full already; my husband and I were very content. Truth be told, I was enjoying being the only girl in the house. Then it happened; I had a dream! (My husband gets very nervous when I relay my dreams to him because of the history of those dreams becoming reality.)

One winter while I was doing a lot of work empowering women, I had a dream of a little girl with dark hair and dark eyes. Given the fact that we already had three biological boys, and I was "done" having children, I wondered if that little girl was partly me remembering my childhood and exposing some difficult emotions I couldn't express. At the time the dream didn't feel significant, . . . until it happened again a few months later.

In the second dream, the same little girl was there, but this time I was talking to my husband, who was standing in the foreground. I remember telling him, "Ken, it's August, and we need to make a decision because the kids go back to school next month." A few months later, I met a little girl who fit the description of the girl I saw in my dream. Only, in real life she simply took my breath away. Her dark eyes sparkled with her bright smile, while her long brown, curly hair bounced with every step she took. I knew it was her.

After a brief conversation with my foster-parent-friend who was with her, we were propelled into two years filled with prayers, questions, babysitting, and sleepovers that proved to be not only respite for the foster mom but also learning about the world of a girl. We spent a summer attending foster care classes through a local adoption agency, since we were uncertain if we were to be foster parents for her, if needed. We took time to pray and discern what our next steps should be. We also heard that it was unusual for someone to take foster care classes and not immediately commit to fostering a child. We didn't have peace to commit to anything but what that little girl needed. Our situation seemed unique, and we found it a little humorous and relieving that our hearts were already tightly knit to her heart.

Eventually, through a series of events, my husband and I both came to full agreement that we should pursue adoption. We began to make more concrete plans for the adoption in the second summer of our relationship with her. The legal proceedings were underway, and we scheduled the home study to begin on August 1. That's when the second dream became a reality! We were now faced with the question of when to have her move in, since the other children were going back to school the following month. That statement from my dream made complete sense. It was August, and we needed to factor in the start of school!

If you know anything about foster care, adoption, trauma, transitions for children who have experienced trauma, or all of the above, you know that many decisions must be carefully thought out to minimize triggers and allow the process to move forward smoothly. The following six months were filled with remodeling our home, equipping our family, and having lots of conversations so we could make room for a beautiful and precocious four-year-old girl.

Throughout this adventurous journey, we have learned a lot about ourselves, individually and collectively. We have learned about our local foster care and adoption systems. We have also grown in our understanding of prayer, trusting God, our community, how amazing all our children are, and how proud we are of each of them. We continue to see God's handprint on this story of ours. and that's what inspires us to want to share our journey with other parents.

Why I wrote this book

Several years ago, a bouncing baby girl came into this world. A few short years later her story would take a very sharp turn away from her first bond of love. Like a tree ripped from the ground when it is little more than a sapling, this little girl was removed from her home and placed in foster care. What followed was some time to heal and grow in the soil of a foster home. And then, like a tree transplanted into new soil, she was adopted by a loving family who had grown to love her during her many visits in their home.

Nobody knew, at the time, that many of the roots of this little girl were damaged beyond repair. This family did everything they could to provide a stable, trustworthy, loving, and safe home for this child. They saw this as a way of swaddling her, as one would an infant, soon after birth. Yet, her emotional wounds were so entrenched in her heart that she refused to accept their efforts. Over time, and after much prayer and counsel, the parents felt as though there was no other option but to consider finding her birth mother.

Fast forward to a few months after her thirteenth birthday; through the help of their local adoption agency, they were able to locate and have a conversation with the birth mother. To everyone's amazement, the conversation went exceptionally well. Over the next several weeks, there would be countless texts, phone calls, and Skype conversations. And soon plans were being made to introduce this not-so-little girl to her first love. Two months to the day later, the once tearful toddler who had experienced such a deep loss when disconnected from her first love was reunited with her birthmother as a precocious teenager. This time the tears were of joy and relief for all involved.

The year, 2017. The family, ours.

You know how many parents say, "I would do anything to help my child heal!" We also used that phrase and made a decision that seemed foolish in the eyes of many fellow parents. While it was a difficult decision to make, we knew it was right for our daughter. Reuniting her with her birth mother would be the one gift that would help her blossom. Just weeks after the reunification, we graciously received these words from her: "I love you both and am truly thankful for what you did for me." Her sentiment was genuine. We could tell because of how deeply we had known and loved her for all those years previous.

I know this isn't the case for all children, but in our story, this was the decision that would send her into a journey of deeper healing and reconciliation. Not only with us, but with others in her story. Her pain was being redeemed day by day.

Sometime later, I mentioned to her that I wanted to write a book about parenting and possibly tie in some stories about the adoption. Here response was, "I think that's great! If others can be helped by our story, that would be great!" Since then, in many ways, she has become my cheerleader. Why is that important? Because as a child I didn't have many cheerleaders, and to receive this blessing from the child I had learned to love became the outcome I had longed for but didn't realize I needed. Her words were a healing balm for the places in my heart that had been wounded.

Although I didn't deliver this little girl through my womb, on that day she was delivered from my heart and into the hands of the one her heart longed for!

This book is appropriately titled *I Am Third: Redeeming the Pain* because I am a third child in my family, and I am the "third" parent in our daughter's story. This journey of parenting both children from my womb and another one through adoption has been a process by which much of my childhood pain was redeemed. There was so much to acknowledge, relinquish, and receive, all of it allowing me to heal in deep places. Let me be clear that I didn't have children so I could heal. Our children became the healing I wasn't aware I needed. Through our brokenness came beauty, and I hope to capture it for you in a way that propels you to grow forward in your story, as well and to seek the hope and healing you desire.

I wrote this book for you . . . and for me.

#LiveYourStory

[**Disclaimer:** *I use the Bible as a guideline and a foundation for my life. I want to acknowledge that I am not expecting that you, the reader, have the same belief system—or any other one, for that matter. However, I do hope that the words penned in this book will somehow find their way into your heart and encourage you in your story. My desire is that reading this book will give you the hope, the encouragement, and the tools you need not only to survive your journey but to thrive in it as well.*]

1

I Am Third

It was in the fall of 2007 that a little girl with dark hair and dark eyes came to me in a dream. Only a few short months later, she showed up in real life with the same long curly tendrils and brown eyes that would make the hardest of hearts melt. Her smile and energy lit up the room and made me forget where I was for a moment. Even her name caused me to question some connections in my personal story, while at the same time I was experiencing a deep joy and inexpressible peace when I was with her.

Two years later and through a variety of ups and downs, we became the adoptive parents to this precious four-year-old. This new role of being mother to a girl would challenge my parenting as a mom of boys. Being her mother also made me the "third mother" in her life. There was her birth mom, a foster mom, and now me. However, the full reality of this "third position" was a few years in the making; it took that long for me to understand that there was nothing "simple" about it. Although my being third was a fact from the beginning of our relationship, it didn't really sink in until almost four years into the adoption.

It was somewhere during these four years that I heard again the story in the Bible about two sisters, Rachel and Leah, found in Genesis 29. Rachel was loved and chosen by Jacob, while her sister, Leah, was passed over and rejected by him. Leah was the girl nobody wanted. She was "weak in the eyes," an idiom meaning that she wasn't particularly attractive. Even though she was older, she ended up living in the shadow of her sister. Jacob desperately wanted Rachel and desired to marry her. Because that culture said that the older daughter was to be married first, Jacob was manipulated by Leah's father: to his chagrin, on the wedding day Jacob was given Leah instead. More than disappointed, he was filled with rage when he discovered this injustice. He had his heart set on Rachel, but he had to settle for second-best in

Leah and then had to wait another seven years before he could marry Rachel. During the years that followed, Leah did everything she could to earn Jacob's love. But unfortunately, she never truly received his favor or attention.

Along with the many emotions I experienced after hearing that story, I also received a gift that day. In many ways, I identified with Leah. I too, was a second daughter who lived in the shadow of my older sister, and for similar reasons. I often lived with the implied message of my being less desirable, less beautiful, and certainly less intelligent. The upside of this was that it gave me a deeper compassion for others who also feel less desirable based on their life stories. Our daughter was no exception. This story of Leah propelled me to pursue a journey of spreading hope to others who feel unloved, and it would begin with our daughter and our other children.

For a variety of reasons, our daughter and I faced many challenges in this mother-daughter relationship, post-adoption. One of the main challenges was that I was not her biological mother. In the adoption world we refer to this dynamic as "attachment issues." Although I didn't fully realize the impact of the story of Leah in my life at the time, it still gave me pause. Just as Leah had felt with Jacob, I was soon able to admit feeling "passed over" by my daughter. This perceived rejection triggered memories of all the times I had felt the pain of being "passed over" and ignored since childhood. Once I acknowledged my own hurt and pain, I was able to implement the lessons from the story of Leah into my own life.

In our daughter's life, I stood in line behind two other mothers prior to me—her birthmother and then her foster mom. My position as "third mom" was challenging for me since I felt the daily rejection of not being completely accepted by her. I would have to learn to "wait my turn." This reality of the three mothers in our daughter's life ran deep in her and caused both of us much pain, since I was not the mother she desired. Her childhood trauma was now being revealed more clearly for me.

In a very personal and intimate way, I would learn to live into my "place" in line. But then the question came: "How do I stay in line and still be the mother God wants me to be?" From the moment that question came to me, it has been at the forefront of my heart and mind. I was going to have to learn *not* to force myself into her space and her heart; I would have to learn to wait my turn. I knew I couldn't do this in my own strength. I was going to need an extra measure of patience and perseverance to endure whatever this chapter in my life was going to hold. I needed to learn to understand how to parent a child who didn't want to learn from or accept me. It was going to be a tough road ahead.

As she grew older, I began to share these lessons I was learning with our daughter because I knew she was also looking for answers in this relationship. I finally told her that, from that day forward, I would live into the title "I Am Third." She was a smart girl with a deep sense of understanding of spiritual things, uncommon to most girls her age or coming from her life experiences. Looking back, I think this awakened in her a stubbornness, a defiant spirit, and a strong desire to fight to get her way through very unhealthy means. I think that my sharing the story of Leah and the lessons I was learning challenged her own life and reality. I didn't mean to add to her pain. I thought I was doing the right thing at the time. Looking back, I think I gave her the right information, . . . though perhaps delivered at the wrong time.

A few weeks after my sharing my insights with our daughter, I received confirmation in a very clear way that I was on the right path. The ministry team at our church decided to host a ministry fair, complete with booths and t-shirts for the leaders of the various areas of ministry to wear as they staffed the booths.

On the front of the aqua t-shirt (pictured on the front cover of this book) was the phrase "I Am Third," and on the back "J.O.Y.," which stood for "Jesus, Others, Yourself," suggesting that, as we serve, we will experience great joy as we are place ourselves third behind Jesus and others.

When our daughter saw me wearing the t-shirt, she gave me one of her all-too-familiar angry faces. At first, I didn't understand why, but then I realized what was happening and was blown away by the connection. She thought that I had asked for the shirts to be printed that way to make a point to her. At that moment I experienced a barrage of emotions and thoughts, from "This wasn't my idea" to "Wow, thank you God for the reminder!"

As challenging as it has been, I continue to stand firm on the idea that "I am third." I stand confident that God will continue to show me the steps He wants me to take in this position. I stand trusting that God will work in our daughter's heart to receive the deep love I have for her amid my own imperfections and the brokenness I bring to this God-ordained mother-daughter relationship.

For taking this stand I have also been judged by other parents. They assume that I am not loving my daughter the "way a mother should." To them I want to counter, "When did you become the expert in my story?" but instead I point out, "Adoption love looks different from one situation to another." You adoptive parents know what I am talking about.

A seasoned mother and fellow adoptive parent in whom I often confide helped me navigate this complicated relationship by encouraging me to ask myself the following questions so that my love would be aligned with my daughter's needs. These questions help me get back on track in challenging times.

Am I being patient and kind?

Am I being prideful?

Am I being rude?

Am I being self-seeking?

Am I being easily angered? (my personal red flag)

Am I keeping a record of wrongs?

Am I delighting in evil?

Am I rejoicing with truth, or am I feeding lies?

Am I protecting?

Am I trusting? And choosing to trust God for her?

Am I hoping?

Am I persevering?

That kind of love never fails.

I had to discover that, when my anger started to get out of hand, I was not being content with waiting in line. Each day I needed to choose to lean into my commitment to parent this child in the way that seemed best for her. Like many other parents, I was willing to do whatever it took to help our daughter heal. Even when this meant acknowledging my pain at being third.

In one of my journal entries, dated October 2015, I wrote the following:

The mystery of adoption for an adopted child can look like a boat between two shores. Living in the boat of sadness, longing to go back to the shore you came from. You don't want to get out of the boat even though your new parents have you anchored at a new shore. You long for the lost parent. It seems that when you stay sad you feel the most connected to that parent.

You believe you deserve hatred. When you feel sad you feel connected to your first mother. That is okay. Your feelings belong to you. They aren't right or wrong. You eventually learn that it's what you do with them that counts. But you still don't want to get out of the boat.

Your new parents and other loved ones do everything in their power to entice you out of the boat and onto the new shore, touting the excitement and the adventure that will come with this move. But the sadness keeps you bound to the part of the boat farthest from the dock, closest to your first mother. You feel as though you will betray your first mother if you give in to the kindness of the others. After all, your belief is that you weren't worth keeping, so why would these people want you anyway? You scowl at their gestures of love and acceptance, and because they have the title of "Mom" or "Dad," you hold them responsible for what your birth parent did in your story. The painful association to your past has the title of parent.

So, what do you do?

You stay in the boat. You find solace in your sorrow. You comfort yourself with the most minute of memories that you desperately hang on to because that's all you have—or so you believe.

You want to ask about pieces of your story, but you fear that knowing might be more painful than the actual separation of your first bond.

Even though you keep being told that "We don't know what we don't know" in an effort to comfort you (there will always be details none of us knows), in the deepest parts of your soul I believe you don't want to build on the pain you already feel. After all, you believe "It's all bad anyway."

But I try to assure you in the simplest way, "I know not everything that happened to you is bad. There are some good pieces. Perhaps my efforts will lure you at least to the front of the boat, where the ladder is.

"Climb out, dear one. I will hold your hand." I motion you to the ladder to show support and comfort for your pain, in the hope of freeing you from the chaos in which you somehow seem to find solace. Even though on the surface you don't want me to know your real self, I think that deep inside I already do. I know you want to be free. I know you don't like to feel trapped. I know you want to be safe. I know you want to be accepted. I know you fear being loved because you've been told, "Your first mother loved you." To you that's just weird because someone doesn't give away what they love. You continue to rest in the lie that you did something wrong to deserve having been abandoned. Right now, for you, being in the part of the boat closer to the opposite shore feels the safest.

I wonder if I am supposed to join you in the boat and walk out with you hand in hand. I don't feel equipped to do so, and I fear I will say or do the wrong thing. I don't want to disrupt your sacred space. I want you to be strong and take the steps you need to so that you can be proud of the strength and insight that reside inside your heart. I don't want you to be stuck in your sadness, but I also don't know how to join you in it right now. I believe I am supposed to stay on the shore and allow you to come out when you are ready. Forcing you has never been an option. Yet sometimes I want to.

Today, it is more important that I ask you, "What do you need from me?" You once again say, aloud or through your silence, "Nothing." But I have come to understand that look of longing you show me. It is all about your love and longing for your birth mother. I am sorry I cannot be who you need me to be today. I am Third.

HOW ABOUT YOU?

What is your "position" in your child's life?

How do you handle rejection?

What does waiting look like to you?

How do you show love to your child?

2

Parenting 101

Three simple and powerful words to help your family build a healthy parenting structure: *boundaries, consistency, follow-through*.

Before I go any further, I must admit that I have never been a fan of statements like "Do these three things and get amazing results" or "In three steps you will achieve what you want!" However, if you commit to implementing these three words as you love your child(ren) and build the structure in your home, I can guarantee that you will have healthier children and an overall healthier family environment. It worked for us and countless other parents we know.

I personally love boundaries because, first, my middle name, Seema, means boundaries. Second, boundaries help protect me from another person's negative attributes, behaviors, words, and expectations, while protecting them from any negative emotions, reactions, or responses I might have.

Boundaries can be confining for some people, causing them to feel as though their freedom is being stolen from them. However, when executed appropriately, boundaries can be extremely effective in helping individuals feel seen, heard, and engaged in the process; this dynamic works in either direction (boundaries can be developed by either the parents or the children).

I like to teach that boundaries are like a window and not a wall. I believe that we were created to live in community, so that during challenging times we may be able to "see" each other. When there is a wall between two people, the chance of other negative behaviors being present increases, and we can't perceive where we stand with the other person.

With regard to parenting a child with challenging behaviors, it is important for the child to be seen as a whole person, beyond their behaviors. It is also important for the parent to model healthy solutions in navigating challenging behaviors. In the early years, I struggled with responding in healthy ways. It wasn't because I didn't want to but because I was still unlearning unhealthy patterns from my own childhood. When there are clear boundaries in relationships, a clear path for communication can ensue; walls, on the other hand, block any form of communication and can misinterpret words and actions.

Healthy and agreed upon boundaries also empowered us as the parents to remain unified in our approach, whatever situation was at hand.

Through a series of events, we realized that we needed professional help to navigate the challenges we were facing. The counselor was very direct when he told us that we were not understanding each other's boundaries. He observed that I had "firm" boundaries, while Ken's were "porous." He went on to explain that porous boundaries leave children feeling less secure about their choices, narrative, and identity. This is even more true for strong-willed children.

Even though my firm boundaries made expectations clear and achievable, the counselor cautioned me that they had the potential to leave the child(ren) feeling unloved, making them inclined to rebel and. consequently, making our job even harder. We walked away realizing that, in some situations, Ken had to firm up his boundaries, while I had to loosen mine. It took a lot of practice, but the transition was smoother than we had thought it would be.

Learning and implementing our boundaries has been a great asset not only in our parenting but also in our marriage, friendships, extended family, work-related situations, and a variety of other relationships and situations.

Since change and growth take time, we need to be *consistent* with our children. When we are consistent with our expectations, responses, choices, or whatever, we are teaching them to expect the same thing as they grow into adulthood. Consistency encourages a healthy dependability and a sense of calm in the children because they know what to expect every time for positive or negative behaviors or reactions.

Seasons of parenting can be very full of a variety of tasks and responsibilities, and if one or both parents is working outside the home, the life of the children has the potential to feel less predictable, unless there are solid structures in place for them. That unpredictability can lead to fear and anxiety in the child and a growing anger and frustration for the whole family. That was the case in our story. I was unlearning old patterns while implementing new ones and didn't realize that the transition was causing me to be unpredictable in some situations. My experience of growing up in a home with more unpredictability than consistency propelled me to crave consistency even more.

I believe that being consistent with boundaries encourages stability. I practiced making my "yes" a yes and my "no" a no. This was harder for my husband to practice because of his porous boundaries and, at times, his lack of patience when it came to dealing with the strong-willed children. There was no room for guessing what I meant. I had to be consistent. both for me and for them. Whether I was at home with the family, out with my friends, or at work, being consistent became part of my nature.

"It's hard to be consistent!" I have been told on more than one occasion while mentoring countless young mothers. I first agree and empathize with them and then remind them that it takes *a lot of* practice but that the return on the investment in the lives of our children is priceless. Many things in life are hard, but if we don't learn to overcome difficulties, we will continue to miss out on what is meant for us.

I will admit that my ability to be consistent also had a negative side. This trait has sometimes robbed me and the family of fun. In our home we had a "school night" routine and structure in place, but when Friday night came I had to force myself to chill out about consistency in our routine so we could all have a little added fun. Don't get me wrong, I love to have fun, and we often did in our home, but when it came to schedules, structures, and responsibilities, I found it hard to not be consistent with the original plan.

Being consistent almost always leads to follow-through. When we are consistent with our actions, we are more apt to follow through in doing what we said we would do.

I'm sure you have heard the phrase "Life happens," right? I am here to tell you, it does! Parents understand better than anyone else that, as we make plans and arrangements, "life happens" and we can't necessarily follow through with what we have said we were going to do. Then we have the challenge of explaining this to the children. Because my boundaries were too firm sometimes, and I struggled with trading in consistency for chill, I would talk the situation over with Ken to gain a different perspective of the boundary I had initially set. I was learning to be a grace-giver to my children, and sometimes that meant checking my boundaries and then approaching the situation differently.

On a smaller and yet more significant scale, follow-through on discipline for a child is not just important but crucial. For example, if you said that the toy, car keys, or privilege (whatever applies to their age and season of life) was off limits during a two-day time-out, then put it in timeout and keep it there for two days. Don't change your mind because their behavior improved within one day. You said two days, and follow-through with that expected consequence encourages delayed gratification and helps them manage their emotions and self-regulate where needed. Take time to help them relate the situation to their emotions and feelings so they will be empowered through the process, and you will maintain a healthier relationship with them.

As with boundaries, I was strong with follow-through—almost to a fault.

There were times when I told a child what the consequence were, only to find out, following a conversation with my husband, that this was an unrealistic consequence. I needed a way out without showing that I wasn't following through with what I had said I would do. The follow-up conversation with the child usually started with, "I was thinking about what I said the consequence would be, and . . . ." I learned that, even if I couldn't follow-through with a consequence, I would at least communicate to the children as best as I could.

All of that said, one of the biggest challenges in our parenting journey was the core difference between Ken and me in terms of our boundaries. From predictable boundaries comes the ability to practice consistency and follow-through. As a result, he became the fun parent, while I was deemed the strict one.

When one of our sons became an adult, he revealed that he had always known exactly when to go to which parent to get what he wanted. Ironically, he also said that, if he didn't want to do something, he would ask me because he knew I would say no, thereby leaving him off the hook for the decision.

I smile today as I key these words, but back in the day it was incredibly frustrating for me that it took Ken a long time to develop and follow through with consistent boundaries. He has since become more and more proficient with boundaries, consistency, and follow-through.

Follow-through needs to be embraced and executed by other family members, extended family, babysitters, and others in the lives of your children in order to promote security in their narrative. Otherwise, they will learn mistrust instead of trust and might grow to be adults who do not value follow-through, causing challenges in their own lives and for the next generation. This is true for boundaries and consistency as well, in order to develop the hearts of the children in healthy ways.

"How does this work with strong-willed children, who are so challenging?" parents have asked us.

Boundaries, consistency, and follow-through are not only important for all children, but in the life of a strong-willed child or a child who carries trauma in their story, they are even more crucial. These three words, when implemented effectively, have the following outcomes on those relationships:

1. Provide a greater sense of safety and security.

2. Encourage genuine support from parent(s).

3. Build reliability and trustworthiness.

4. Help rewrite the narrative for the child carrying trauma.

5. Empower both parent and child(ren) to understand and live into their strengths in healthy ways.

6. Provide order to a rather chaotic and challenging family environment.

7. Give stability to the family, and especially to the strong-willed child.

Motherhood is a beautiful privilege and blessing; however, when our firstborn demonstrated a deeply rooted strong will, I wasn't sure I wanted to have any more children after him (I am glad I did!). I have heard it said, "Most of our mistakes are made with our firstborns, so we should be sure to apologize to them the most!" I fully agree and have certainly apologized many times over the years!

When our daughter joined our family, demonstrations of her strong-willed nature often pointed back to the effects of trauma in her story. At other times her innate stubbornness was clearly at work. Discerning the different reasons a child may be presenting as strong-willed is crucial because behaviors based in and resulting from trauma must be carefully handled.

I may not have realized it at the time, but I am very thankful now for my experiences in raising our oldest son. I wasn't always proud of how I handled situations, but I learned a lot about myself, including recognition of my many unresolved thoughts and feelings from my own upbringing and how they affected my parenting. Truth be told, I was not a strong-willed person, as some might think, but learning how to differentiate my will from my strong personality, while parenting strong-willed children, took some work over the years.

During a rather difficult season, when our oldest was just a toddler, my mentor shared a book with me; it was titled *You Can't Make Me, But I Can Be Persuaded* by Cynthia Tobias. In her book she stated, "You can take a horse to water, but you can't make it drink. . . . BUT you can salt its oats!" Wow! Was that ever a game changer for me!!

This powerful quote has stuck with me over the years, and it is one I apply in a variety of situations. The horse won't drink the water just because you bring him to it, but if you salt his oats, he will be *thirsty* for that water! The same would be true while of the situation while parenting a strong-willed child; translation: "Find his price tag!"

This inspired me to find ways to encourage our strong-willed son to be "thirsty" for obedience. Not in the monetary sense, but in terms of ways in which we could learn what really mattered to him. If something did indeed matter to him, we would find creative ways to get him to comply and cooperate. This was a long road, but we found many small ways to achieve the goals of maintaining a healthy relationship with him, teaching him self-management and self-regulation when things didn't go his way. All of this, needless to say, while simultaneously practicing self-control and self-regulating ourselves as the parents.

It wasn't till he was in his late teens that he began to value and respect himself, us, and others, in the way we knew he was capable.

Our Parenting Philosophy

Whether the children are biological or adopted, we believe the same principles apply:

1. Parenting is as much about the child (his or her bent) as it is about the parent (his or her bent).

2. Recognize the child as a unique individual, created and wired for a specific purpose.

3. The child is not you—so just because something worked or didn't work in your childhood doesn't mean it will work the same way for your children in your parenting journey.

4. Encourage biological children to practice empathy and compassion for the adopted children. For example, when your biological child has experienced rejection, ask them a few questions like "When have you felt it?" "What did it feel like?" "How did you respond?"

5. Remain unified as a couple. This takes work, but it is crucial in building a solid foundation.

6. Acknowledge birth order to understand the children's tendencies.

7. Learn to discern and work with particular challenges. In our situation these were based on three categories in our adoption narrative: (a) girl, (b) relinquishment issues, and (c) disobedience. Learn to recognize and identify such distinctive or compounding issues in your own experience, so that you may respond appropriately when issues come up.

8. Some of the initial needs of adopted child(ren) include (a) learning and adapting to your expectations regarding truth telling and hearing, (b) learning and adhering to the language and expectations of your home, and (c) safety and security.

9. Encourage empowerment. Whether the children are biological or adopted, allow them opportunities to grow responsibly, and don't do for them the things that they can do and the things that they are supposed to be doing (take age into consideration). Beginning with the end in mind will help them launch successfully. (Adoption resource: *Adoptees Coming of Age* by Dr. Ron Nydam)

10. Allow your faith to inform your parenting.

11. We can't give our children everything we didn't have in the hope that our own pain will be diminished in *their* story. Instead, we need to pass on the lessons we learned from those shortfalls.

12. Learn about and respect the "culture" and generation your children are growing up in.

13. Maintain healthy boundaries in your home to build safety and trust.

14. Encourage autonomy to reinforce a strong sense of belonging.

15. Validation and affirmation are key to nurturing a healthy identity.

16. Learn from your history and make necessary changes by which the lessons will apply more effectively to your children.

17. Realize the impact your diverse family is having in their story, and help them navigate the many challenges they might experience outside the home.

18. Equip the children with tools they will need to navigate their adult worlds.

19. Provide a home and family structure they can be proud of.

20. Celebrate the small wins in yourselves and your children.

HOW ABOUT YOU?

How effective are your boundaries (if you have them)?

In what areas do you struggle with being consistent?

What does follow-through look like in your story?

Are you a strong-willed (stubborn) person, or are you parenting a strong-willed child? How is it going?

3

From Familiar to Foreign

This chapter was inspired by the book *Foreign to Familiar* by Sara Lanier. In our case, parenting has been a journey that has taken us from *familiar* to *foreign*. We were biological parents to three sons before we became parents to our adopted daughter.

Sara Lanier's book helps individuals learn about similarities and differences among various culture groups and what one might experience when traveling overseas. It is also a great resource for those of us who are in interracial relationships, whether in a marriage or a friendship and any relationship in between—helping us recognize the foreign and become familiar with it. The author does a fine job of describing and explaining the cultures in a way that is easily understood. As a cultural coach, I have referred to her work often to help individuals understand culture more effectively. This is not the place for a full book review, but I will leave you with this: "It's a great read if you are a person who is open to embracing diversity and learning about cultures while stretching your mind to be more inclusive."

Although Sara's premise was to draw the familiar out of the foreign, her book inspired me to articulate our journey of adoption in the opposite way. We went from the *familiar*ity of parenting three biological children, in our case sons, to experiencing the *foreign* relationship in adopting and raising a child from the local foster care system—and that, too, a daughter.

Many well-meaning fellow parents tried to convince us that parenting an adopted child would be just like parenting our own. First, it is not. Second, they did not seem to understand that we considered *her our own*, too.

Learning about her story and being a student of how *she was created* felt like a fulltime task. With our biological children, although I was a student of them as well, in many ways I felt as though I already knew them because of how I knew myself and my husband. I knew our story, and I had a visual framework of their features and personalities. Learning how to embrace a child who was born from another woman's womb had its challenges, to say the least. So, I would have to first surrender the notion that *I was her rescuer.*

Parenting a girl was foreign to me, since as a "boy mom," as many labeled me, I didn't have any experience doing so. I quickly learned that looking at her would force me to rise up in courage and acknowledge the hurting little girl inside me. I needed to discern whether her responses and reactions were based on "girl, sin, or trauma" and then respond accordingly on a case-by-case basis. I had to learn to restrain myself when receiving questions and comments like "How can you adopt when you can't handle the three you have?" or "She isn't your real child." And the hardest advice byte of them all: *"Just love her."*

All of these and more were foreign to me when she joined our family.

I did love her. I do love her. But nobody told me that she wasn't going to *receive* the love as easily as our biological children would. I did not think that she would struggle with trusting me, since I considered myself as trustworthy and reliable with our other children. Yes, that was humbling.

I did not know that her trauma would trigger the need for me to wrestle with the lies I believed so intrinsically or the negative comments I had received in my childhood as a daughter. I did not realize the ache I carried in deep parts of my heart till her pain became a mirror for me. It felt all too familiar.

And then there is the question of "home."

Why didn't she feel "at home" with us, as our biological children did? Why did our home feel foreign to her, and what were we going to do to make it more familiar? These were just a few of the questions we were asking to help us navigate this aspect of parenting an adopted child.

In the early days of writing this book, we were celebrating with our friends who were preparing to move overseas. The question of "home" came up with some of the guests at the gathering.

More specifically, the question was "Where is home for you, and how do you define it?" Several responses were worth pondering. From the simple cliche of "Home is where the heart is" to deeper responses such as "acceptance and familiarity," so much truth was shared, based on who it was who was sharing. It was certainly a thought-provoking conversation, and one that set us on a track to becoming more intentional about building familiarity for all of us in our home.

For me, the definition and context of home have changed over time. Of course, for me as a child, it was with family. A home geographically shifting from Pune, India, to Ontario, Canada, to Michigan, United States. Home for me entailed lots of cultures, lots of people, lots of experiences, and a growing need and desire to redefine the reality for me because of some personal challenges I faced along the way. I longed for true connection to the *place* and the *people*.

As I grew into my college years, friendships, and eventually marriage, "home" began to look a lot different. It felt transient to me, and for good reason. The more I got to know myself and others around me, the less comfortable I felt with certain people and in some places. Even the union of marriage makes us think that we have a "new and permanent home" outside the single relationships we had crafted. I love my husband and am very glad we married each other; it's the marriage-into-a-culture-I-wasn't-familiar-with that often became the challenge. That isn't a dig against my in-laws or their culture—it's just me realizing that I had a lot of learning and growing to do in the context of my interracial marriage. Even though I felt at home with my husband, I didn't feel the same about his culture or his group of extended relatives.

For me, home is *people*. I feel most at home when I am with people who provide a space that shows that they see me, hear me, and are not afraid to be truthful and genuine. Most importantly, they are emotionally and physically safe. This understanding and realization opened a door in our story at which I began to discover where or why our daughter did not feel at home in our house. I discovered that *home* was people for her, too.

Her deep inner longings nagged at her, while on the outside she observed a family trying their hardest to provide familiarity and a home she could be proud of and share about. I know this because of some conversations we have had. We made as many changes as we could to accommodate her needs but reconciled ourselves early on to the fact that she might never feel totally "at home" with us. Even though we believe we did our best, the question of *Are we okay with that?* lingered in our hearts and minds.

The answer was always *No!* so we were committed to keep trying, no matter what.

HOW ABOUT YOU?

How do you handle "unfamiliar" situations in your story?

Where is home, and how do you define it?

How does your cultural bent/home impact your parenting?

How would you have gone about building an environment that would have fostered a healthy process for our daughter, had the situation been different? How did you go about this process with your own adopted child?

4

The Tree

Our family moved a lot during my childhood, from two countries and to many towns in between. I had to learn how to acclimate to each of the "new soils" into which we settled. Learning the culture, language, systems, and provisions and understanding those communities would all be part of my learning curve.

Fortunately, we had great support systems along the way. From classmates to teachers to church members who helped in our journey. Little did I know then that those experiences would equip me to provide similar supports for our daughter as she learned to adjust, acclimate, and settle into the new soil of our home.

I recently heard an interesting analogy that helps explain how we are to parent our children who are living with trauma. The woman suggested comparing our adopted child to an uprooted tree—a sapling that has been removed from another yard/field and replanted in our own yard/field. Once the tree is dug up from the soil, the roots need to be covered and kept wet, so they won't be destroyed during the transfer.

The roots need to be protected in the hope that they will take hold in the new soil and provide the tree with proper nutrition and life to keep it growing healthy and strong for many years to come. As we take care of that new-to-us tree, we will water it, weed around it, and ensure that it doesn't get diseased.

The speaker went on to say that, in a similar way, children who come into our family through foster care or adoption could be considered to have been transplanted. We often clip their branches and leaves to shape them. We make sure they get proper nutrition and medical attention, as needed, to help them not only to survive but also to thrive in their new soil. Sadly, many parents cover the roots by hiding truths in the child's narrative. There might be safety issues surrounding that ever-growing explanation as the child matures, but in many cases the birth parent(s) was reacting out of fear of rejection or other unresolved brokenness in their own stories. Her strong encouragement was that we focus on the roots. This sounded like an interesting picture to me, so I found myself reflecting on it the next day.

When I think of how our child became available for adoption—this part of the story is common to many cases—I acknowledge that she is indeed like a young tree ripped from the original soil of the only home she had ever known. She was protected by the authorities, yes, but that trauma had lasting effects to the core of her being.

When a child is transplanted into the soil of another family, we all hope that he or she will bond and attach to what the new family holds sacred to their narrative. Just like the protection of a tree and its roots, the new family, as best they can, needs to provide protection for the child's roots. As with any human being, when we are ripped from those we love or experience trauma in any way, the effects are not always noticeable till later in life.

I know that we did the best we could to protect her roots once the transfer happened, but over time we realized that many of her roots had already been irreparably damaged and wouldn't attach to our soil or to the relationships in our home. This frequently left us feeling as though we were attempting to force attachment.

After reuniting her with her birth mom a little less than a decade later, we noticed strong signs that she had in fact attached to us. Not always emotionally, but through strong appreciation of values and beneficial lessons learned during her time in our home. Her desire to connect relationally with us and her brothers seemed intentional and inviting, a new and welcome effort on her part. This new transition in our story proved to be incredibly healing for all of us.

During the writing of this book, my husband and I relocated to India, my birth country, after we had successfully launched our children into adulthood. We made a mutual and willing decision to sell our house and all our belongings and relocate with nine suitcases to our name. However, this transition has also caused great pause and reflection in my story.

I initially left here with my family at the age of five and have lived in either Canada or the USA for the past forty-eight plus years in a variety of soils. There are so many layers to my story, but the one strong connection I make to our daughter's story is this: Ken and I were both reunited with our childhood soils. The only difference is that she needed a better place to heal, and I came back to my childhood soil as a healed and redeemed woman.

Redemption and healing are for all of us, even though when, where, and how we choose to receive it might be different for everyone.

HOW ABOUT YOU?

Do you have trauma in your story?

How have your roots impacted your story?

Where and when have you had to acclimate? What did you learn?

5

The Impact of Culture on Trauma

As a woman of Indian origin who grew up in the western culture for most of my life, I didn't realize the impact that culture had on trauma until our daughter joined our multiracial, multicultural, and multiethnic family.

From a racial standpoint, we said that she blended right in because the combination of her brown genes (Hispanic and African American) and white genes (maternal grandmother) had given her a skin color similar to that of our biological sons. This often allowed her to feel as though she fit in, even though she didn't yet feel as though she belonged.

Her ethnic features are unique to her Hispanic and African American heritage and very different from my Indian ones. However, when people saw us all together in those early years, they often thought she was of Indian descent. When the reality of the differences was stated openly, this caused uneasiness in all of us, because it might potentially mean that she didn't feel seen. It was my job to celebrate her distinctive features, even though sometimes they caused her to remember her past and everything she'd lost.

When it came to marriage, in our home the work that was needed to understand each other's cultures was just as challenging. When we got married, I was specifically told by a white person that we would face challenges because of our different races. However, that was never the case. Our true challenges came through learning to mesh our cultures together. The cultural challenges we faced in parenting our daughter also included the cultures of foster care, adoption, and trauma, as opposed to being limited to her ethnic background. While we learned about her needs and cultural preferences, we tried to help her unlearn some things that seemed to have left scars on her heart.

I carry cultural trauma in my story in the form of social pain. Social pain occurs because of interpersonal rejection, loss, or bullying. On many occasions I have experienced these against my race but, more specifically, against my culture. I was bullied as a child and then again later on in my adult years by other non-whites in my community who didn't understand or appreciate my desire to be a bridge-builder with white people. I also experienced cultural trauma at the hands of friends and family members who didn't want to take the time to explore my culture. I was often told, indirectly or directly, that being "different" was wrong. At times the pain was unbearable, and I couldn't even talk about it outside our home. Experiencing loss became commonplace for me because I would either lose the potential friend due to their lack of understanding or have to walk away and lose the relationship because I wasn't willing to endure the constant rejection.

When I first moved to the USA and married into the Dutch culture, I did whatever I could to fit in. Because of a desire to belong, I lived into many expectations from friends and family so that I would be accepted, plain and simple. Many years later I discovered that I had lost sight of who it was I was created to be: an Indian woman with a mosaic of cultural beauty in her narrative. For me growing up in the states, most of that mosaic was ignored, not only by others but by myself as well. As I began to tune in to this reality, I started to pick up in conversations that cultural diversity wasn't acceptable.

I was once told by a member in our faith community at the time, "My parents think it's great when people adopt children internationally but said that if I fall in love with someone who isn't white, they will have a problem with that." My face held an expression of horror since Ken and I are obviously in an interracial marriage. I wondered what they thought about us. As our conversation continued, I asked whether they realized the truth about us, that we were obviously an interracial couple. It was made very clear that the parents of this individual didn't see color since they had decided I was now Dutch by marriage. Granted, this happened around thirty years ago in America; although there have been more efforts on the racial front, the work of understanding culture still has a long way to go. (Please visit our website at seemaglobalconsulting.com for more information on our Understanding Culture workshops.)

Up until the adoption of our daughter into our family, Ken and I had done a lot of work to understand his Dutch American and my Indian-Canadian cultures. We wanted to maintain a healthy, well-rounded family experience for our children and ourselves. Our adopted daughter added her beautiful combination of Hispanic and African American to the mix, so we were excited to add her cultural traditions as well.

In the early months and years adding traditional Hispanic dishes to the weekly menu, inviting our Hispanic and African American friends over for a meal, or visiting cultural festivals were all great ideas. We believed that those opportunities gave our daughter a sense of familiarity amid all the changes she was experiencing in her new home with us. Over time, however, we noticed that she exhibited many negative behaviors surrounding those experiences. After some conversations, we realized that those experiences were reminding her too much of her childhood and birth family and that she wasn't quite ready to "go there" yet.

The topic of culture has always intrigued me, and I have always wanted to ensure that those from other cultures feel included. This started with my family. So, to see our daughter experience such pain at my attempts to make her feel included caused me to pause and take a deeper look at what else might be going on.

In our Understanding Culture workshops, I unpack the experience of living cross-culturally and give tools to the participants on how to maintain a sense of wellbeing while doing so. Living cross-culturally could mean moving to a different country from the one you grew up in or simply engaging in relationships in which the other person is different from yourself in terms of race, ethnicity, or culture.

Over time, living cross-culturally can cause a person to experience any or all the following: frustration, misunderstanding, confusion, tension, embarrassment, and aggression. A nurse friend of mine told me that these are also considered the six pillars of grief. So, in essence, when our daughter felt any of these coming from me I was adding to her grief and loss. This didn't minimize the trauma she carried in her story, but the cultural dynamic would make things worse if I didn't take the time to understand them in detail.

Whether it is family culture or ethnic or racial culture, the message is often the same: "This is how we have always done it." Sadly, that very message, despite some possible redeeming qualities, can feel very confining to others if the intent is not clarified. When it is used to oppress another person, that makes it even more detrimental.

Granted, there are recipes from generations past that need to always be prepared in a certain way. There might even be some cultural traditions that bring great joy and celebration to an individual that they want to pass on to others. It gets tricky, though, when a cultural nuance is lived out in the form of "This is how we have always done it" with *no room* allowed for the other person's uniqueness or need to be understood.

How do I know this? I am guilty of doing the same thing! In many instances I have been guilty of either using that phrase or insinuating it in our family—whether the context involved house rules, parenting techniques, or food preparation. In my defense, I still made room for someone else's opinion, but I certainly preferred "my way." But there were signs that my parenting style was causing our daughter a lot of pain. That was a tough one to swallow because that was "how I had always done it." I was very comfortable raising our sons, so I assumed the same approach would work for our daughter. I was wrong. I needed to be more creative and more sensitive to her unique and specific needs.

For instance, being direct is one of the cultural nuances I brought with me. It's not just a personality trait; it's deeply rooted in my cultural background as well. My being as direct as I was made it difficult for a child to receive; this applied especially to this one who carried deep woundedness, combined with her strong need for control. My directness was wounding her even more. Although I had done some personal work on my approach with our sons, I had to learn to temper this tendency even more with our daughter. Why? Because it was impacting her trauma in a negative way, and that did not sit right with me. I did not want to add to her trauma in any way or to be part of the problem, since I was committed to being part of the solution. As time went on, her story was shaping my own story more and more.

Another cultural norm is that Indian culture is highly relational. So, it sits at the core of my personality and gives me joy to connect to different people; this helps to expand my world every day. When parenting a child with significant broken relationships in her past, I came to recognize that it was hard for her to trust and build relationships again. We can't expect our wounded children to just jump on board, as I did, and have a positive, thriving relationship. This will take time, creativity, and patience, . . . if it happens at all. I desperately wanted a positive and healthy relationship with our daughter, and most days I was probably trying too hard, which left me depleted, since I wasn't seeing a return on my relational investment at the time.

In both these situations of being direct and being highly relational, I was being challenged to "be different" and to "not be myself." This challenge continued to perpetuate the belief that I was not accepted. However, as I journaled, prayed, and had long conversations with my husband, I understood that I wouldn't necessarily need to change *me* but that I did need to pay attention to how I approached situations and articulated my thoughts. I gained new perspectives without losing sight of myself.

With reference to cultural, ethnic, or racial nuances, many people think they must change who they are to fit the other person. I don't believe that is necessary or helpful. I believe that we have all been "fearfully and wonderfully" created and have been given an opportunity to offer our unique selves to this world. So, live your story.

When I first got married, I didn't cook much Indian food, didn't wear Indian clothing, and didn't speak Hindi. Only through the years of acknowledging and healing from the negative impact the Dutch and American culture clash was having on me did I find the confidence, joy, and excitement to pursue who I was really created to be. I am grateful for a husband who protected and supported me in my healing journey. We saw the same change in our daughter as she grew in her own understanding of who she had been created to be. She eventually fell in love with the connections with which she felt comfortable.

As a result, we all grew forward together!

Here are suggestions on how you can be more intentional in relationships when the other person is different from you, no matter how they have entered your story. Because in the end, inclusion enhances belonging!

- Understand your cultural narrative.

- Make room at the table (of your story) for people different from you.

- Ask questions and learn.

- Step into the mess with them.

- Show acceptance of, not just tolerance for, the differences.

- Don't force assimilation into your way of thinking or doing something.

- Be a student of the other's culture. Then show that you are learning by implementing ideas.

HOW ABOUT YOU?

How does your culture impact your story?

Are you experiencing social pain? If so, when and how are you handling it?

How is inclusion viewed and expressed in your story?

6

Name Chang(er)

Names change for a lot of reasons: marriage, adoption, preference, or even entry into the witness protection program.

After all, what's in a name? Identity? Character? Meaning? Legacy? You tell me.

So, what happens when a child's name is changed after adoption? Do they lose any of those things I just listed? Maybe, or maybe not. Is a name really that important? When I raise this topic, please know that my comments are in reference to older child adoptions.

When my husband and I got married, I chose to take his surname. This gave me an Indian first name and a Dutch last name. I was proud to take his name but wasn't ready for the comments I would receive over the years. We lived in a city with a large population of Dutch folks. "You're Dutch now, with that last name!" people would say with a proud smile. What amounted to an insensitive and ignorant comment on their part seemed like a total disregard for my feelings and a complete lack of cultural understanding. On many occasions, when I met someone in person after talking to them on the phone, they would have a shocked look on their face to see a brown woman with a Dutch surname . . . and no accent. I again wrongly assumed that these Dutch folks knew that there was a subgroup of Dutch called Dutch Indonesians, who have darker skin.

Once I learned to overcome the countless racial and cultural microaggressions I experienced, I tried to turn some of them into humor. Basically, I learned to expose my unusual reality before it was spoken by the other person. I remember distinctly, before delivering a motivational talk to a room full of mostly Dutch women in West Michigan, that I said, "Don't let my last name fool you; I am not Dutch." This was my attempt to break the ice in a humorous way. Some laughed, others gasped, and then there were some who just did not get it.

When we were in the throes of the adoption of our daughter, our caseworker asked, "Do you want to change her name?" My immediate response was "No!" I felt as though I would be betraying her, her birthmother, and her narrative somehow if I did change it. You are welcome to your perspective, but, in all honesty, I have struggled with parents changing their non-infant child's first name while finalizing their adoption. My opinion gets stronger if the motivation was one or more of the following reasons I have heard from some parents: "We preferred the name _____ for our son" or "I've always wanted a daughter named_____." And then there's this one: "People won't be able to pronounce her name." With our daughter, we were sometimes asked, "Don't you want to shorten her name since your last name is so long?"

Understandably, some children need to have their names changed for security and safety reasons based on family history. When a child is adopted from infancy, I have heard that some parents make the given first name the child's middle name for some of the above-mentioned reasons.

As part of my research for this book, I spoke with some adult adoptees to find out their perspective on name changes. Some said this signaled a loss of identity and honor with regard to their birth parents. Others said this change brought about a second detachment from those birthparents after the sting of the first separation and relinquishment. A few even questioned whether they had full and unconditional acceptance from their adopted parent when their original names were changed.

Sadly, because of the relinquishment experienced by adopted children, many of them carry along a suitcase full of grief, rejection, brokenness, confusion, and a variety of other emotions. Since their undeveloped brains are challenged to withstand the pressure of assimilating into this new "forever family," they are flooded with deep and sometimes painful feelings about how and where their story started. This can certainly add to the already challenging road for both parent and child to travel. A name change might negatively impact the adoptee's ability to attach to their new family.

When I met our daughter for the first time—long before we adopted her, I was shocked by her first name. Her name contained my father's name within it, and since my relationship with him had been distant to nonexistent for most of my life, I did not want the reminder of him. This was another painful trigger in my story and another opportunity to overcome a challenge. Later, I looked up the definition of her name and found to my amazement that it means "God is the winner, full of favor and grace." With her carrying a power-packed name like that, I was certain we were *all* going to be okay! Years after the adoption, I wrote the name and its meaning on a whiteboard and hung it in her room—for her and for me. I needed a constant reminder and eternal hope that would carry her . . . and me . . . and all of us through this journey.

Titles are also a part of many names, and sometimes how they are used or who uses them determines the title as well. So many people have great titles . . . with no character or lifestyle qualities to back them up. For me, the title *Mom* was close to my heart. I took it seriously, sometimes too seriously—to which my children and husband can attest.

Our biological children lovingly call me *Mom*. When our adopted daughter joined our family, she struggled with this. I tried to understand. Really, I did. But instead, I took her reluctance as a personal slight, until one day I recognized the longing she had for her birthmother. I too had longed over the years for a closer connection to my mother, and our daughter's beautiful brown eyes were tainted with the same pain I felt in my heart.

This situation forced me to learn the difference between *adoption* and *relinquishment*. Adoption is the positive act of bringing a child into a family permanently. Relinquishment by the birth parents, while physical and legal, can be seen as an act of releasing from, leaving behind, of giving over possession or control of. Relinquishment for a child, if it even happens, can be emotional and may even be replaced by reluctant resignation. I assumed that, since we had adopted her and provided a loving, two-parent home, our new daughter would embrace me well. I did not understand the depth of her grief caused by the relinquishment, or that having a new "mother" on the scene was not going to make all her pain and loss go away.

Amazing how a little learning and a change of perspective moved all of us onto a new trajectory. From then on, her pain and struggle to call me Mom made sense. I surrendered the title of "Mom" and found the courage to allow her to call me "Mrs. Kinita" till she felt comfortable with the more familiar name and its implications. I chose to change my "name" so she could continue her healing journey. I realized that her healing and our relationship were more important than my title.

It is important to acknowledge that, for some people who have been adopted, the word *adoption* conjures up more pain than the person would like to admit. For many children who are adopted, that label is a constant reminder of the pain of what may have been for them a reluctant relinquishment. Yet for others, it is the best gift they could ever have received. Adoption doesn't end the brokenness in a child or fix what someone else broke. Sometimes adoptive parents incorrectly believe that it will. Adoption may help write a new narrative filled with healing and growth that the child might need. But sometimes it doesn't.

HOW ABOUT YOU?

What does your child's name mean to you?

How do you view relinquishment and adoption?

How do your spiritual beliefs contribute to or diminish your ability to parent a child who is dealing with the pain of relinquishment?

How does your faith model, if you have one, inform the healing process?

How are you helping your child(ren) find security in their identity?

What role does your faith community, if you are part of one, take in supporting your parenting efforts with biological, foster, or adopted child(ren)?

7

Not Chosen

This journey of adoption has me experiencing a myriad of emotions, many I am not proud of or able to make sense of. I continue to feel restless on this journey of parenting a child who doesn't seem to want me. This continued rejection feels directly pointed at me. I am beyond exhausted. (My journal entry in 2014)

Over the months and years, I wondered whether anyone else who parented an adopted child felt the same way that I did. Were there perhaps other parents on a similar journey? If so, where were they? And why were we not talking about it?

I can't help but refer again to the story of Rachel and Leah. Leah experienced ongoing rejection. Her solution was to have children in the hope that Jacob would accept and love her the way she needed and wanted. In some sense, I was also guilty of birthing creative methods to get our daughter to love and accept me. I discovered that this was a heart issue . . . and by that I mean an issue of *my* heart.

As time went on and after many failed attempts, the realization grew that I was not going to receive her acceptance. Instead, all that my struggle was fostering was anger in her and disappointment in me. I wondered when I was going to learn—not just realize, but truly learn, that she had needs and desires that did *not* include me? As much as I knew this intellectually and tried with everything I had to accept it, the truth was that my own scars from the rejection in my younger years were being reopened daily. I thought I had healed, but I found myself really hurting inside. Can you relate?

As a parent, I often asked myself what I was doing to allow the perceived rejection to continue. Was there a way to stop it? Was I reinforcing the message that *"It was okay to abuse me,"* since that's how it felt to me? Why couldn't I remember that her behavior toward me had more to do with what was going on in her heart than with me specifically? What could or should I do? These and many other questions would fill my thoughts throughout each day.

Most people, including us, believe that adoption comes with many blessings, and although that is true, it is also true that, as with any relationship, it has its challenges. However, the root of those challenges isn't often with an adopted child entering the new family; it begins with the relinquishment that occurred before the adoption. Relinquishment, as the term applies to the child, is what the child experiences when they come to grips with the reality that they must leave their first family behind. To relinquish means "to voluntarily cease to keep or claim; to give up." In order for an adoption to be possible, a relinquishment must take place. It took us a while to embrace that reality, since we had been living with only half the truth—that adoption is a beautiful blessing. As soon as we embraced the truth that the relinquishment was the root of her pain, I immediately started to search for answers on how I could partner with her in her growth. Little did I realize it at the time, but this choice would serve as a significant growth opportunity for me as well.

At that point in my life, I had put in countless hours of personal work in my story. Through this process of parenting our adopted daughter, I became aware of a new layer to my narrative. I realized that, not only did I personally struggle with attachment issues when our first child was born, but now I was staring into the face of the ugly truth of relinquishment. I began to wonder whether the two were somehow connected.

I grew up in a two-parent home with my birth parents and biological siblings, and adoption was not part of my narrative. I commit that to writing because, many times in my adult years, people have thought that I was adopted since I was born in India but grew up in Canada. Yes, living cross-culturally has had its challenges, but I wouldn't trade the experiences for anything.

Throughout my childhood I received messages of rejection from a variety of people and situations, messages that shaped my heart and thoughts in negative ways. I began to equate rejection with relinquishment. It never dawned on me that my experiences of rejection would bring me to a place of questioning my ability to attach, . . . until our daughter joined our family. This was a worthwhile process for me to undergo, and I eventually discovered that I didn't have a problem attaching to others—though I did have a problem with my sense of being rejected and pushed aside. Truth be told, I far too often felt the pain of not being wanted and thought that some people in my past had simply given up on me. As we learned more about relinquishment, adoption, and the brokenness people live with as a result, my pain seemed insignificant compared to theirs, and my heart expanded with compassion and empathy. Then one day, I found that I could honestly say that "our daughter's pain became my pain—the pain that I was called to carry with her."

My pain from rejection was serving as a catalyst for me to show acceptance and not just tolerance of other people. I learned to use the energy it took to harbor pain and lack of acceptance and instead focus on the betterment of our daughter's life and the lives of our other children. I realized that I was guilty of tolerating all of the members of my family and not genuinely accepting them and their faults. I believed that my children would accept me no matter what—and they did and do—but the adoption revealed in me the brokenness I still carried deep in my heart.

As I took inventory of what was in my heart, I continued to forgive those who had rejected me in my past. This also meant forgiving my native culture, in which girls aren't respected or valued. As I continued this work of forgiveness, I found myself in a stronger and healthier place to respond to all of our children in the way they needed me to. I also found a new purpose in becoming someone equipped to advocate for girls' and women's empowerment.

As I was walking through this process, I allowed a trusted friend to walk with me in that painful place. She kept encouraging me to not take it personally, to not let the "digs" and attacks from our struggling children affect me so much. She would remind me that they were acting out of their own trauma and brokenness. Although I had heard this explanation before, it hit me differently this time, and I admitted that I was responding to her out of the remnants of my brokenness.

Taking time to reflect on and understand my childhood pain made me realize that our daughter's narrative had become a mirror image of my own early story, and I didn't want any part of that old me! Yes, I had my own triggers, but I was healing and needed to empower her in the same way. To focus on her behaviors and not on her heart would add to her trauma and would only serve to repeat my history in her story. I wanted all of our children to realize that I was rejecting the *behaviors* (and the old me I saw in them) and not *them*! Sadly, I think, our children thought I was rejecting them when I wasn't. It was difficult to navigate all those emotions, for sure. Our daughter's struggles and pain were triggers for me back to a time and place that no longer existed in my life, and I wanted the same hope, freedom, and joy I now experienced for her. I wanted her to embrace a heart space where pain and restoration could reside simultaneously. I believed that, since I could do so, anyone could.

I turned to a trusted mentor to get answers, and she counseled me to "guard my heart." I often heard her gentle voice amid the screaming questions and wonderings during that season. She reminded me that "feelings aren't right or wrong, they just are!" She suggested that, even though the rejection felt real to me, I needed to remember the truth that God had chosen our daughter for us. She told me to speak truth to my heart and remember and embrace the truth about my children and anyone else who made me feel rejected. Perhaps they were speaking through their own brokenness as well. Did the Old Testament Leah ever learn to guard her heart? Was that the solution? My mentor assured me that it was but cautioned me that the process would be difficult. Yet she also reminded me that, since my narrative was full of difficult and challenging situations that I had learned to overcome; I could do it again.

So, I became intentional about guarding my heart. What did that look like?

- Journaling.

- Acknowledging the hard feelings and giving myself permission to feel them.

- Prayer.

- Surrender (letting it go).

- Putting healthy boundaries in place when dealing with toxic and difficult people.

- Reminding myself of "truth" statements.

- Learning to trust God on behalf of the other person.

- Truly believing that "not everything is about me"!

Even though rejection was something I thought I had learned to overcome years before, this time I reframed the issue with more confidence that propelled my way forward. Little did I know at the time, but the practice of guarding my heart would help me immensely in many situations going forward. I learned to apply this strategy not just in parenting, but also in friendships, family dynamics, and racially charged incidents and encounters that I experienced with strangers and people in my community. And the list goes on.

Guarding my heart against rejection also empowered me to deal with the anger that was growing roots in my heart and taught me to overcome other hurtful emotions as well. Guarding my heart also gave me the strength and ability to guard my daughter's heart more intentionally. It gave me the opportunity to embody the strength she needed when she felt weak, and it helped when we needed to make decisions about issues that were beyond our control. I finally found a way to turn the perceived rejection into something positive and more productive, in both her story and mine. Even though I often felt "unchosen" by her, I didn't want her to feel the same pain that I was experiencing. Guarding her heart meant first guarding mine so I could help her and not hinder her process.

During the time we were seeking more help for our daughter's healing, we sensed that we needed to reach out to her birth mother. Although we can say now that the reunification was a success, we did not know then what was going to happen. We faced many unanswered questions before we decided to move forward. Questions such as "Is the birth mother safe for our daughter to be around?" "Are we disobeying the law, since ours is a closed adoption?" "Will exposure to her birth mom help or heal our daughter's heart, or will this exposure make things worse?" "Will we cause a renewed sense in her of rejection from us?" and many others.

I want to ask you, are you in a similar situation? Can you relate to our situation? Maybe you have other questions. Where do you go to find answers?

I know that I was chosen for her, and she for me. But the truth is that her tender heart wasn't yet ready to embrace our relationship as a gift. I would need to wait my turn yet again while I learned to guard my heart.

HOW ABOUT YOU?

How do you handle rejection—from the child(ren) or perhaps from others?

What does being chosen mean to you?

How are you guarding your heart in your current season of parenting?

8

The Library

A library is a place that holds books, ranging from stories to research materials. It's definitely a great place to build creativity for children; it helps them expand their world and their dreams. "The past is our library," is a phrase that sends me into a pool of many thoughts and feelings. Our past serves as a library as we remember, reflect on family stories, and reminisce on where we have come from. This library is filled with the good, the bad, and the ugly. Each book is this library is a smaller chapter of a bigger narrative.

Some of us have so many chapters bound by brokenness, fear, and trauma that we would prefer to simply burn them all in a bonfire. We don't even want to think about it. While others might have books upon books of primarily sweet memories and healthy relationships. Most families have both, and I have come to realize that, as good and positive as many of the books might be, there are no perfect families or people in this world—including my own!

When I first heard the phrase "The past is our library," I was triggered back to memories of my past . . . including what actual libraries meant to me. When I was growing up, the local library was the place to *escape*. I would hang out there on a Saturday and do homework or work on a "made up" project just to get out of the house and away from all the chaos. However, while I was there for the day, I would often peruse the comic book section while I sat in a La-Z-

Boy and listened to music with large headphones on. It was a safe place, frequented just to pass the time and find some much needed peace. Yes, I would do homework, but my day often included people-watching and diving into my backpack of snacks that I had snuck into the library with me.

I figured that this childhood book in my library was just another story in my narrative and wouldn't really make a difference . . . until I had my own children. It soon became apparent that some of the books on the shelf of my past were going to negatively impact my husband and my children and that it was time to face them head on. I remembered a time when our children were small when a friend invited me to go with her and her children to the library to get some books. I froze. I realized for the first time that the years of escaping to the library weren't something I wanted to encourage in my children. Somehow, I was now supposed to help them experience the library as something positive.

Unfortunately, the trigger to "escape from chaos and stress" wasn't resolved in me at that moment. My early need to escape, along with all the emotions experienced when I did escape to the library, were all at the forefront of my heart and mind. But I had a decision to make. I didn't feel ready for this. I didn't want to impact my children in a negative way. So, after confessing to my friend the struggle I was having, I asked her to take our children to the library for me. She was glad to do this for the first couple of times. After a while, she empowered me to come along and suggested an exit plan in case the experience proved too difficult. I agreed. I did use the exit plan that first time, but never again.

All the bookshelves of our past will look different. There is not a one-size-fits-all, and that is okay. For those of us who are parenting children who were not born in our womb, this can be a very challenging road to travel because, in essence, we don't know the intricate details of the child(ren)'s history before they joined our family. We only know what we were told by the agency that handled the foster care or adoption process. Sometimes those details are vague or worded so positively that we can be shocked when the truth does come out.

Whether your child came to you through foster care or was adopted as an infant or a teenager, domestically or internationally, they will have an extensive library in their past, one that could potentially hold many answers found in the deeper stories from the child's library.

Adoptive parents need to be students of their adopted child so they can be the strongest and most honest teachers in their lives.

It is up to us as parents to step into that library and learn as much as we can, so that if and when they ask questions, we can give them accurate information that will help them heal and put the broken pieces of their story back together. The better we understand what's in the chapters on their shelves, the better we will be able to handle the information and share it with our child as needed. Learning about their narrative in detail will also help parents utilize various resources, as needed, to help them grow and thrive. If you didn't learn many details about your child's history, start now if you can. It is important for us as parents to help our children identify the roots of the pain and struggles they face. But that means we need to go into their libraries and help them discover what might be lurking in the shadows of their hearts and minds. This work is necessary for our biological children as well, so that when they get older we can give them clear reference points in their narrative to help them in their journey.

Adoptive parents need to be students of themselves so they can be the healthiest and safest advocates in the lives of their child.

Please remember that it is crucial that we understand our own past first. For example, how do you handle chaos in your own life? How have you handled pain and trauma from your past? You might be thinking that you don't have trauma in your life, and perhaps that is true. The fact that you have not experienced trauma in your own life, however, might put you at a disadvantage in dealing with your adopted child's trauma. When you hear or see the effect of trauma in your adopted child, what has been your first reaction? Don't let a trigger from your child's trauma be the first time you address long-buried trauma in your own life. Your child needs you to be healthy enough emotionally to have some answers and to experience and demonstrate empathy, understanding, and patience.

For years I have carried a painful experience that happened in my story when I was between seven and nine years old. I was once again reminded of it when we were teaching our daughter some self-management tools at around the same age. I recalled some stressful emotions in my heart and mind. Once I processed this with my husband, I realized that these emotions were triggers to the memory of what had happened to me. The good news was that I wasn't debilitated by the memory any longer and was able to use the opportunity to empower our daughter. The subject we were talking about was a sensitive one, so understandably I had some emotional response surrounding it. However, once I identified the *why* behind the emotions, the memory from my story was void of all vestiges of the trauma I had once experienced.

So often we run to the nearest or most popular theory, book, article, or therapy and then do our best to apply this insight to our child, when we might need to look at ourselves first. Yes, it is always good to tap into resources around us regarding specific issues we are facing in our foster care or adoption journey. I want to encourage you to pay attention to why you get frustrated when some of those ideas don't work with respect to your child. You might need to do some work on yourself first.

My faith has also played a vital role in growing me as the adoptive parent our daughter needed. I didn't always get the action steps correct, but I always believed that this child had been hand-picked to be our daughter and that we had been hand-picked to be her parents. This gave me the hope to keep growing forward and learning as much about her as I could.

In closing this chapter, I want to remind you that there isn't a one-size-fits-all strategy or approach for parenting, whether this be parenting an adoptive or biological child. It is necessary for us to get a deeper understanding of the chapters and books in our library, so that we can be the best parents we can be for our adopted child. I found that I was a more effective parent once I acknowledged the root of the triggers in my story before attempting to help her with hers.

HOW ABOUT YOU?

Do you escape *to* your past and keep reopening the books that line your shelves?

Do you escape *from* your past and ignore the books that line those shelves?

What emotions do you experience when you visit your past? Freedom? Or fear?

9

Being a Student

Whether or not we admit it, our children teach us. They teach us lessons and correct us, directly and indirectly. We should experience change by what they teach us . . . for the good and the bad. What is your child teaching you? How are you being their student?

In my early years as a young mother, I quickly learned that I could not parent alone. That I needed to submit to my husband's ideas for some solutions so we could attack the challenges of this adventure together. I felt insecure and ill-prepared and was afraid of making a mess of it all as I stepped into this new calling in my life. Some unresolved issues and negative messages from my childhood were impacting my marriage and parenting in ways that were unhealthy and unhelpful in terms of helping me to grow forward in those roles. With the help of a counselor, my husband, and trusted parenting mentors, I started to uncover the deep hurt and obvious anger I was carrying in my story.

So much of what I learned at that point was by trial and error.

Then it hit us—the reality that there have never been children like ours on the planet, because they were the ones we birthed. The DNA from the combination of a Dutch/American man and an East Indian/ Canadian woman and the physiological and cultural makeup of each of us would play a unique role in our story. Combine that with our adopted daughter's narrative, and we had lessons we would carry well into our empty-nest years. Once we truly embraced *all* of that, we started to grow forward as a strong family.

Not only was I growing as a student of my husband, but now together we learned to be students of our children. We didn't always get it right, but we were consistent and followed through with ideas that, more often than not, had good results.

Parenting has grown me in ways I did not see coming. It was a vehicle that taught me how to be the business owner I am today. Parenting revealed my strength (see the chapter titled "Knowing

Your Strength" on page 103.) It exposed many of my weaknesses, both spoken and unrecognized. It challenged me to grow; to slow down; to listen better; to be present; and, ultimately, to always keep fighting for those I love.

Parenting has taught me that pain can be redeemed. Weaknesses can turn into strengths, or the strength can sometimes be outsourced. Hard work, consistency, and follow-through will pay off in the end. Being honest with yourself and others will always lead to healing and to a deeper sense of accomplishment.

Our kids have taught us to be forgiving and to keep reconciling so we can grow forward together.

Children make good and bad choices all the time. At the precious age of four, our son confirmed the strength and depth of his strong will. We realized at the same time the strength and depth of mine. He chose to deny that he had cut his own hair; after a long period of questioning, his conclusion was, "The scissors jumped up and cut my hair." His reality was not received well by me, but I accepted it even though I am a mother who is passionate about truth and justice. I realized that in his mind there was some truth to what he was saying, peppered with denial. He was living his reality, while I was living mine. That gave me yet another opportunity to forgive him and reconcile within myself *my tenacity* to push for truth and justice.

They have taught us that it is okay to be scared and yet share openly with each other.

When one of our son's was in high school, he came to me with a question I was not prepared for. The topic was taboo in my culture, and as the parent of an opposite-gender child, I was extremely nervous about how to handle the question. I was secretly wishing he would have had that conversation with his father instead. But I managed to stay calm, chose my words carefully, and did not allow my emotions to get the better of me. To be completely honest, I was petrified that we were talking about it at all. However, grappling with that one question made our bond stronger in that moment, . . . and helped prepare us for what we would face down the road.

I once heard that parents should "listen to the small things when the kids are little, because when they grow older, they will come to you with the big things." Based on the above story and that son, that prediction came true.

They have taught us to be intentional in staying connected.
From running errands to just sitting around in the same room together, staying connected can happen through a variety of venues. We have all been in situations in which we disconnect from our parents for one reason or another. Sometimes that is part of growth and development and trying to figure out our identity, while at other times it is because the dynamic in a relationship is unhealthy. I have often expressed that "staying connected wasn't a family value" while I was growing up. Perhaps it was a value my parents had; if so, I did not experience it. So, we chose to be more intentional with our kids.

They have taught us how to love deeply and genuinely.
"I love you" or "I am proud of you" were not assertions I heard while growing up, but I knew how important they were and made sure I took every opportunity to say them to my children. Especially once I had broken free from the impact of negative messages in my story. The more I articulated those sentiments, the more I *wanted* to say them. I did not want our children to have the same emotional holes in their story as I had in mine. I experienced the redemptive power of love and the words and actions we use to express them.

They have taught us how to be unapologetically authentic!
From the beginning, Ken and I had the understanding that children were to be raised to be good citizens of their communities and adults with integrity and good character. Encouraging them to have faith in God by setting examples and good teaching was at the core of how we grew our family. We wanted them to be "unapologetically authentic," so that is how we attempted to live our lives. We believed that, even though there were many things we taught our children, there would be many more things "caught" by them as they watched us. Being a parent is a high calling, not for the faint of heart. Our kids are watching. They are watching us, and they are watching other parents around them to help them navigate the world in which they find themselves.

All that to say that our children should not become clones of us. They need to learn to be their true, authentic selves. I am not saying we should not celebrate our commonalities; I am saying that we do well to let them make decisions they are comfortable with. We need to *understand* that the consequences are theirs and not yours. Unless, of course, we have started them on a track of encouraging bad choices. We are to *teach* them to live into their strengths, while coming alongside to support them in their weaknesses. To *share* openly and vulnerably where we are not "getting it right" and to work together for an age-appropriate solution. To *learn* together so we can grow forward together.

I must admit that there was a season for me as a mother when I was prone to live by an implied "What you see is what you get!" and "I am mother, hear me roar!" I am here to say that this approach was not conducive to healthy relationships with my children, my husband, or my friends. If I could turn that tendency around, so can you!!

"We need to ask our kids to teach us."

Asking our kids to teach us shows that we realize we are not perfect and do not know everything. It also helps expand their worlds and minds. It sets an example for them to seek help when they are uncertain or do not know how to do something. Are you someone who struggles to ask for help? Your child is watching and learning how to do the same.

One of our sons loved to cook and bake as a teenager. I love to cook, but to connect with his strength I asked him to teach me new marinades and bake for different opportunities. He was also strong with technology and often came to my rescue; this is still true today as I write when he is off at college. Granted, I would often find myself acknowledging, "My brain isn't going to remember this for next time." That was my way of reminding him of one of the needed roles he played in my life.

Another teaching moment . . .

In 2015, I lived through a 7.8-magnitude earthquake in Nepal. Since then, I have done a lot of work on this journey of healing, frequently addressing the post-traumatic stress from this incident that I carry in my story. At the writing of this chapter, six years into my healing journey, I have learned that the body keeps score. A book by Bessel Van Der Kolk titled *The Body Keeps Score* helps people address the trauma in their stories and know how to process it.

When I hear an alarming noise before seeing where it is coming from or determining what is making it, the muscles in my neck and shoulder (where I carry an injury from the earthquake) tense up, and I find myself holding my breath. Once I acknowledge what that noise is and determine it is not threatening, I breathe my way to relaxation. I am thankful to say that the distance between the two is getting shorter.

What does that have to do with parenting? This. Our firstborn is ever so passionate about guns. I do not like guns. I do not like the sound of guns. Can you see where this is going?

I decided to ask our son if he would take me to the shooting range and teach me how to shoot so that, with his help, I could face my fear head on. As a side note, our relationship had been extremely difficult in his younger years, and never in a million years would I ever have thought to ask him to "sit with me in my fear." When he was a child, I was not good at sitting with him in his, so why would he want to sit with me in mine? (This is one of the many things I have needed to apologize for over the years.) He was elated at my request, and we scheduled the grand event right away as a Mother's Day gift. My PTS (post-traumatic stress) responses were in full swing, even though I had extra ear and sound protection. Even my tears were poised and ready to roll as I picked up the gun and put it down again a couple of times before shooting. My son taught me all I needed to know to handle the situation safely, but my body was anticipating the noise even while my heart was celebrating the redemptive healing in our relationship. I did it. I pulled the trigger with my finger and let the tears fall as they chose. All I could hear was my son saying, "Mom, don't cry, it will be okay!"—in place of the sound of the gun.

I knew as a young mother how to handle "situations" safely, yet my heart and mind anticipated the negative messages that reinforced failure as a parent. I was angry, felt deeply, and pulled the anger trigger all too often. I did not recognize that it would be okay if I did not get angry or cry.

Though I will never need to shoot a gun again, I will always cherish the way our son taught me how to be safe, to be confident, and to stay strong. Who would have thought . . . ?

How About You?

How and what are you learning from your child(ren)?

Where could you do a better job of being their "student"? Share this with someone else for the purpose of accountability.

10

Practice Makes Permanent

It all began when I was challenged by a client of mine during my hair salon days almost a decade ago. At the time, we were on the brink of adopting our daughter, and after parenting three biological sons, I was a bit nervous about how to parent a girl. Many of my anxious thoughts about "getting it right" had to do with my nervousness about the possibility of repeating my mother's mistakes and worrying that I would discover things about myself that I wouldn't like. All-in-all, I was scared that I wouldn't measure up to the other amazing mother/daughter relationships all around me. It was a challenging season, to say the least; little did I know it at the time, but I was going to learn a lot!!

Just so you know, I was not very good at nurturing. I continue to be a tell-it-like-it-is, high justice truth-teller who loathes sugarcoating things. Raising a girl made me feel like I needed to work on those areas since I only had practice with boys. My client and I were talking about ways to effectively teach kids, while utilizing their unique learning styles. She reassured me by asking me to finish the sentence "Practice makes _____." Immediately, I responded with "perfect," because that's what I had learned. She graciously corrected me, pointing out that "practice makes permanent." That correction was risky, if you ask me, since I had the scissors in my hands. But hearing that statement caused something to happen inside me. My heart flipped, assimilating a new perspective that was full of hope.

I pondered the idea of "practice makes permanent" for a moment and observed, "So, if we practice the right behaviors and thoughts, the right behaviors and thoughts will become permanent. And if we practice the wrong behaviors and thoughts, then the wrong behaviors and thoughts will be permanent?" Eureka! Little did I know at the time that this connection would not only be instrumental in helping me manage my anxieties around parenting, but also prove to be a breakthrough in coaching and teaching our daughter to manage her challenges. You see, we have all been programmed to respond with "practice makes perfect." What a lie!! None of us is, or ever will be, perfect. As a parent of four children and a wife to one man, I am far from perfect. No matter how hard I try, my weaknesses will always be part of my story. I have spent a lifetime trying to compensate for my weakness while focusing attention on my strengths. But the reality is that I have had to learn to live with them while practicing what works and what is good and right for me.

What I didn't tell you is that this client of mine was a special education teacher. She worked with children who had life-altering disabilities that were not going to be changed by practicing. They would need to adapt to new ways of doing things, where possible, and their parents would have to seek out resources to aid in their skill formation. From that day forward, I chose to practice (to make permanent) what our daughter would need and what I would need in order to become the *permanent* parent our children needed.

So, how do we implement this strategy of "Practice makes permanent"?

For myself as the parent, this meant:

- Consistent time strengthening my faith while on this journey of parenting so that I would be filled with peace and calm for those unexpected moments.

- Taking care of my personal needs (food, hydration, rest).

- Staying true to myself about everything and not covering up my pain.

- Being intentional about taking care of my needs.

- Asking for help and accepting it when it was offered.

- Growing in self-awareness to learn what my triggers were and how to handle them when they showed up.

- Finding and implementing healthy habits that fill my soul.

- Learning to handle life when it doesn't go my way (surrender, aka, letting go)

For the children, it meant:

- Posting 5 x 7 notecards around the house that stated this truth in bold print That made for a great reminder for us parents, too!

- Checking in with the children on a consistent basis to celebrate their progress.

- Discouraging the use of the word "perfect" in our family.

- Encouraging them to keep trying to push through whatever struggle.

How and in what contexts can we reinforce this concept? Here are a few practical examples:

- Drying dishes: We practice putting them back where they belong, so that over time this repetition grows their memory.

- Laundry: We show them how to fold and put their laundry away in the proper drawers to help maintain order. Just so you know, I am in no way a clean freak, but those seemed like practical ways to teach my daughter in particular to manage her surroundings and help her manage her emotions at the same time. And it gave me some help I needed around the house.

- Anxiety: We use healthy coping skills to calm ourselves and help our children discover methods that work for them.

- Anger: We give ourselves permission to be angry, but we find practical and healthy ways to respond *in* that anger. We also seek outside help from a trusted friend or counselor, as needed.

Here are some lessons that I've learned along the way, as we pay attention to this idea of practice making permanent:

- Being *inconsistent* will add discouragement and frustration to your day and theirs.

- Not following through with what you said you would do encourages children to follow suit with their commitments as they grow (the consequences get bigger as children grow up).

- You and your spouse/partner need to speak with one voice. Different styles are to be expected, but the message needs to be delivered with a unified voice.

- Children need to know that we are willing to acknowledge and correct our mistakes and to learn from them.

- Parenting is about establishing good foundations and then continuing to erect more principles and concepts, one at a time, on top of one another as the children grow.

This tool isn't a "perfect" method (pun intended). But it gave me an effective and practical way to reach my goal of healthy parenting. I believe that it was one of the vital principles that changed the trajectory of our parenting experience. I hope it does the same for you!

The first step toward practicing this concept is surrender. Letting go of that over which you have no control. Surrender was something with which I had become very familiar before I had children. So, it came naturally for me to put this into practice in my parenting. Once I acknowledged the root cause behind my holding on to my children so tightly (in a figurative sense), I was able to let them go. There were too many times to count when I "took" a situation back into my hands, . . . only to watch it fall apart in the end. I learned to do my part, to stop listening to the expectations around me, and to practice what I, my marriage, and my children needed me to practice so that we would have harmony and peace in the home. If I could do that, so can you!

Here's to practicing making permanent what your children need, so they can learn to thrive in their stories.

HOW ABOUT YOU?

Do you consider yourself a perfectionist?

What are you practicing that is becoming permanent? Is this helpful or harmful?

What are you willing to surrender in your role as a parent?

What are you hoping will grow because of your practicing?

What are you seeing in your child that mirrors your choices?

What changes are you willing to make in your practices for the sake of your family?

11

Finding Normal

Normal, as defined in the dictionary, means "conforming to the standard or the common type; usual; serving to establish a standard; approximately average in any psychological trait as personality or emotional adjustment; free from any mental disorder; sane."

If you are anything like me, alarm bells are probably going off in your heart or mind right now.

Here's why: I don't conform well to the standard or common expectations of others. I tend to weigh my decisions and actions carefully, considering my own convictions and values. As I read "approximately average" in the above dictionary definition, I must ask questions like "What are the factors that are being considered?" "What makes any human being 'normal,' let alone a child with trauma or loss in her story?" And the rest of the definition? Well, if you are a parent of an adopted child, the rest of that definition is just plain heartbreaking. Because we understand that the struggle is real.

Families involved in foster care or adoption are all prone to trauma and mental illness; physical, emotional, or learning disorders; or other issues that will cause them to struggle and even question their own sanity at times. The stress, chaos, and overall trauma that exist in adoptive families and can include mental illness can also lead to full blown PTSD (post-traumatic stress disorder). Another factor that we had not understood was one our therapist labeled as "Secondary PTSD"; it is consistently found in parents, caregivers, and other children in the home and family of an adopted or foster child. Secondary PTSD is real and can potentially go unnoticed, even though it can sometimes cause us to question our own sanity.

Are any of us parents normal, as per the definition stated above? If your answer, like mine, is "no," then why do we work so hard to get our kids to achieve "normal" status, regardless of how they have arrived in our families?

I have had to learn to grieve the reality that what others consider "normal" may not be who I am and may certainly not describe the situation in our home. While certain traits might be common in someone else's story, the dictionary definition of normalcy might not be accurate for me and my family.

Our stories are full of expectations from ourselves, others, and even the culture we come from or live in. Sometimes, it seems that when we fulfill the expectations of others, we are considered "normal." On more than one occasion, when I did something "different," it was instead construed as "wrong."

Each of us is created uniquely, with a wide variety of gifts, talents, qualities, and personality and character traits. Our foster and adopted children often come with the added ingredient of trauma, resulting in the necessity for the common methods of parenting to be turned upside down. In our case, add to that a multiethnic, multicultural, and multiracial dynamic due to our unique marriage, and we had the potential to create an amazing experience in our family; alternatively, if we had been naive to our children's needs, we might have completely blown it! The need to balance expectations with the specific needs of our particular children takes work and intentionality. We needed to find a system that worked in our own home, one that would hopefully instill healthy virtues and values and encourage a sense of belonging in our children.

As a mother of three sons, I learned quickly that not all mothers of sons are the same. Nor are all families with boys. Thankfully, I never gave in to the comparison game with other families and learned to confidently remain unique with regard to our sons and the dynamics in our home. Although I was very lonely at times, I knew that, as a woman of color who had married into a culture and race different from my own, I had to be sensitive to the needs of our biracial sons and then eventually our biracial daughter when she joined our family.

I needed to be aware of the stereotypes and microaggressions that were operative in our community and country, so that I could equip our children appropriately and help them build confidence and courage into their lives. Many of our white friends who had children couldn't relate to our experience and would often regard their own stories as "normal," while clearly disregarding the distinctive features of our story. There were instances—too many to count—when I had to attempt to help others understand the racial and cultural challenges we were facing as a family. To our disappointment, many people didn't understand. Maybe the reality is that they just weren't willing to try.

As time went on, it became much easier to recognize the signs of trauma and the corresponding pain and rejection our daughter carried. Seeing how trauma impacted her allowed me to focus on grieving the losses *with* her in an effort to give her a childhood she could be proud of. But this also required that I address some residual threads of trauma from my own childhood. Working on my trauma also provided me with the opportunity to give her the tools I had been given and used to overcome my trauma. This wasn't easy, but it was worth it!

Understanding expectations, managing grief, and adjusting my pace to accommodate her needs and the needs of our other children became part of our rhythm as we journeyed forward together as a family. Trauma responses are unpredictable in the early days, weeks, months, or even years of an adoption. So, we watched for patterns, looked for the appropriate resources, studied certain issues, and had consistent dialogue with her counselor. All along the way, we tried to put healthy boundaries in place to help our daughter heal and all of us respond appropriately.

Because of safety concerns in our family, our "normal" consisted of tighter boundaries and added structure that sometimes felt restrictive to us and the other children. While most families were able to "pick up and go" without any concern about the kinds of challenges we were facing, we had to be mindful of potential triggers and ensure that we planned accordingly. Change and transition come hard for some children, and any kind of transition can trigger a myriad of negative behaviors that can escalate without warning. Sometimes a transition triggers a strong memory of separation from the birth mother or birth family, while at other times the situation might be met with a more-intense-than-normal loss of control. Sometimes a smell or image escalates problematic behaviors without warning. Being on high alert became normal for our family.

Because we set some of these boundaries and structures differently from other adoptive families, we were sometimes met with disapproval or a lack of understanding. Besides my counselor, there were very few others with whom I could process my thoughts and feelings. Mostly I was met with confusion, a lack of empathy, or criticism. Parents of foster or adopted children or of biological children with special needs in varying degrees know what I am talking about. I want to encourage you to do your part in making this world a place of healing, unity, and peace for your child.

At the end of the day, the pursuit of perceived normalcy in society or culture needs to be addressed through the lens of "What does my child need in order to be a healthy child today, with the hope of becoming a healthy, thriving adult tomorrow?"

Keeping our children and family healthy means that we as parents need to do our personal work to build a healthy foundation for the children and to put all our family members on a trajectory they can be proud of. Children who grow up in a safe and secure home environment will more likely become adults who function with the same value of safety and security in their relationships and environment.

As a Transformational Coach, I have, over the years, met with individuals and couples who have stuffed, ignored, glossed over, medicated, or avoided the issues from their own childhood. Sometimes, they in turn become parents who wonder why their children's issues are so challenging for them. I cannot stress enough how crucial it is for the parents to address the elements in their own stories that might be causing greater pain for themselves and, as a result, for those around them.

A healthy mindset and a healed heart begin with me . . . and you. Yes, I am talking about self-care. Dear parent, self-care is crucial if you are going to learn to not only survive but thrive. Your self-care methods might not look the same as those of another parent, whether biological or adoptive. But I encourage you to normalize self-care in your story.

For those of you who can relate, I see you, I hear you, and I want you to know that you can overcome and be strong for your child. Do what you need to in order to maintain as healthy a relationship as you can with them, while meeting their—and your—specific needs.

And remember, at the end of the day, "normal" applies most aptly to a setting on the clothes dryer.

HOW ABOUT YOU?

How do you view "being normal" in the context of your story?

What does self-care look like for you?

What issues from your childhood do you need to address?

12

Chosen to Belong

During a particularly difficult season of challenges with our extended family, I wondered why the concept of "being chosen" or "belonging" kept surfacing in my heart and mind. I had the confidence that I was chosen to be in my family, but I always struggled with the "belonging" part. Born a girl in the Indian culture—in my case a second daughter— carried more weight than others understood. My position in the birth order came with challenges that I didn't understand till years later. Because belonging wasn't reinforced in my home of origin, I believed the narrative that I wasn't wanted and didn't belong. When I had my own family, I learned that we as parents needed to establish a value that reinforces that our children fit and belonged. We wanted to create security at home, even though the children would experience plenty of situations outside the home where they wouldn't always *feel* as though they fit in and belonged.

Over the years, as I did my personal work to heal from my childhood wounds, this statement came to me: "I was chosen to give hope and to serve." Our adoption experience showed me that I was now being called to choose and give hope to a precocious and beautiful four-year-old girl, who in turn would be used to teach me lessons of unconditional love and hope.

The word *belong* became a theme of great challenge in our home shortly after we adopted our daughter. That word would stand for an ongoing journey in the direction of clearer understanding, both in her story and in mine. Webster's Dictionary defines *belong* as "to be in the relation of a member, inhabitant (of a family or group), to have proper qualifications, to be properly or appropriately placed."

Our intentionality of helping our daughter feel as though she fit and belonged in our family became a catalyst in my own personal story and revealed elements in my upbringing that I hadn't thought about before. It forced me to revisit experiences that reinforced a lack of acceptance, belonging, and tolerance and pushed me to delve deeper to understand what being chosen meant.

I discovered that the adoption journey is a complicated one and that there is no one-size-fits-all solution for navigating the variety of situations adoptive families face. It became for us an intense learning process. I often found myself intentionally clinging to my faith throughout this time, lacking as I did either solid answers or direction.

The truth is that I could do only so much to help instill in our daughter that elusive sense of belonging. She would need to accept my efforts in order to heal the way she needed to. I couldn't force her to belong. None of us can force another person to belong—a hard lesson for many of us to learn.

Fellow adoptive parents, I am sure you recall a million efforts on your part to "help" your adopted son or daughter weave themselves into the fabric of your family. I know we have. For me, the harder I tried and the more resistant our daughter became, the more my frustration grew. But I also realized two things. First, I saw that she was struggling to belong and realized that our efforts might only exacerbate negative outcomes. Second, and more importantly, I realized that "doing my part" in helping her belong was not going to make her *feel* she belonged. Still, I knew that I just needed to keep doing my part!

We fully believed that she was chosen for our family, and we for her. But we now needed to understand how to "set the table" in a way that would reinforce belonging. We believe that "inclusion enhances belonging," so we became more and more intentional in our inclusion efforts.

While I was doing some research for this chapter, I stumbled upon this journal entry that I had written during that period of time:

Today I asked God to strengthen me . . . and her. This was a scary prayer because it seems as though she is already strong in many ways—some not so healthy. But I was seeking the kind of strength for her that comes through deep healing that only she would be able to attest to. A kind of healing that rests deep in my story and gives me the strength to pursue each day and each experience with confidence and vigor. I asked God to heal her heart and transform it so that she could give a lasting kind of hope to others with a similar story. I ask you, God, to help her release her pain and give her the ability to forgive those who taught her rejection instead of belonging.

Although I had prayed variations of this prayer over the years, at the time I wrote this I didn't see much change in her. However, I experienced dramatic change and growth in myself.

On countless occasions along this parenting journey, I learned the lesson that I was to "be a mom to our children and not their God." I was often in that place, leaning into what I knew to do as a mother and trusting God to work in her heart and mine so that our efforts would result in a positive outcome. I needed to step out of the way.

Our daughter was chosen to belong *in* our family, and the adoption journey taught us all that we belong *to* each other. Belonging to each other reveals the responsibility we have to walk with each other on our good days and on our bad. Being intentional about reinforcing belonging causes hearts to heal and relationships to move forward.

For you parents who are struggling right now with a child who doesn't want to belong, please receive this challenge and encouragement from my heart. I want to stress that it is *your* responsibility to set the table (environment) and make it conducive for your child to belong, but the end result is *not* in your control. Maybe your child doesn't know how to want to belong. Maybe their shame, mistrust, pain, rejection, and trauma are holding them captive. Please don't add anger, judgment of the birth family, criticism in your heart, insecurities, or any other negative response to that list. Trust me, I know. My anger and insecurities were out of control on many occasions, and I am not proud of that. This complication only increased the gap between me and our child and impacted our reconciliation and efforts to promote belonging. Give your child the keys to unlock understanding, freedom, acceptance, and value, all of which have the potential to lead to a deeper sense of belonging, and then release your expectations with regard to the timing of those results. Give it your all . . . and then surrender it.

HOW ABOUT YOU?

What does belonging mean and look like to you?

Are you someone who is struggling to belong to the "family" you are in?

Are you someone who is wondering whether you belong anywhere?

Consider the places you do and don't feel as though you belong. What do you need to do to eliminate any negative thoughts or feelings in this regard?

13

Summer Lessons

For us as parents of four children, it felt as though there was always something interesting going on in our story. Since we didn't have a manual to instruct us, we went with what worked and attempted to correct what didn't. Looking back, I am sad to admit that, for the first few years, we focused on behavioral management instead of trying to determine what was behind those behaviors. At any given time, it seemed, we as parents were either dealing with our own behaviors or one or more of the children's. We thought at the time that we were doing the right thing in addressing their behaviors. But when we adopted our daughter, we discovered that learning what was behind her behavior was a necessary and effective strategy for helping shape her heart and for assisting her in healing from the pain of relinquishment and learning to attach to our family. From then on, this became the approach we took with all our children.

What a learning curve that was for our family. As a result, we had better structures in our home and experienced growth in all our relationships. This might not be a new concept for you, but it was for us—one we learned to grow into. We realized that the adoption was an adjustment not only for us but also for our biological children. It was our responsibility to find ways to maintain our sons' connection to us in more than just biological ways.

One school year, as summer break was approaching, I started to feel extremely anxious about how I would manage the summer holidays. As fellow parents know, having children home from school for an extended period can cause a lot of challenges and hardship for one reason or another. This is more of an issue for children who have personal challenges beyond their control, due to their trauma or disabilities. Because schedules change or there is a significant transition, we need to expect challenges and recognize that certain problematic behaviors will escalate.

I was thankful to have learned how to navigate the transitional challenges we faced with our oldest son when he was a child. However, since we were committed to shepherding our children's hearts instead of focusing only on behavioral management, I had to be more intentional about the structures, expectations in our home, and the specific needs each of the four children had. I needed and wanted tangible solutions that would help us all grow forward.

The summer following the first year when all four children were in school full time was the first summer we experienced some major challenges related to transitions from a highly structured school routine to a summer routine that was somewhat looser at home. The good news was that the situation revealed a pattern. Each week of that summer, I considered a particular word that described what might be going on in our adopted daughter's story. Over the course of that first summer, I compiled a list of words that would come in very handy for helping her heart heal and would provide healthy structures and responses in our home. I kept a copy of that list (noted below) where I could refer to it often. Each word was a descriptor of what might be behind the behavior that our daughter was exhibiting. I knew that if I learned to provide what she was lacking or struggling to obtain, I could help her in tangible ways. But if I just addressed the behavior, the result would be short lived.

This list of words gave me a "handle" on how to proceed. The need to address these words showed up during holiday breaks in a variety of ways as well. The list helped us all find some order in a world too often characterized by chaos and pain. I was also able to understand behaviors at school from the lens of this list, resulting in improved understanding and communication with the teachers and administrators at the school. I was finally feeling like the advocate for our daughter that I was called and wanted to be.

By way of whetting your appetite for this listing of words, I share with you some of my journal entries from that first summers of discovery and the two that followed:

2013: *We are discovering words that are clarifying what is behind her behaviors. Every week they have shown up as a "theme" from her behaviors. I am learning so many lessons through her triggers, and how they are revealing mine.*

2014: *A full summer of the words from last year, and, somehow, I wasn't surprised by them. I have a long way to go but am proud of the way I am executing proper responses.*

2015: We just finished our third summer since we learned the words and have been practicing them during the school year too! We can all see that they are losing their power and that she is learning to overcome the issues. I am not anticipating the behaviors anymore; I am just executing the responses. It is almost as though "seeing her heart" has become second nature to me. I am glad she is responding well to this process because I now have PTSD from the traumatic experience of being in an earthquake earlier this year. Thankful to have more order in our home while I try to heal personally.

Below, as promised, is the list of words, along with a description of what each word meant in the context of our daughter's story. Following the descriptions are practical approaches that worked for us; it is our hope that they may help you and your child rewrite their narrative. I am not minimizing the pain and trauma experienced but am seeking to identify what could be behind certain behaviors. I will also try to share with you options for positive outcomes. I found that this was empowering for our adopted daughter and for me because it gave me clear direction. I couldn't fix her emotional pain, but I could equip her with ways to overcome her struggles and not allow *them* to overcome her. Your list might look different, but hopefully some or all of these ideas and approaches will give you hope in your journey of parenting:

1. **Control**: Helping her understand the impact of having it and then losing it.

   - I gave *choices* for just about everything, at least wherever I could.

   - Whatever choice our child made, this gave her confidence one way or another to feel a sense of control in a healthy way.

   - I showed and spoke empathy if the result of her choice wasn't what she had hoped for.

   - Parents, please remember that setting an example of how we handle ourselves constitutes a learning lesson we aren't necessarily talking to our child(ren) about.

2. **Responsibility**: We empowered her in this by encouraging self-care and care for things that belonged to her and others.

- As a child in the foster care system, our daughter learned that adults outside her family were responsible for her needs and choices and made all the decisions for her.

- On a positive note, we are thankful for a system that shows up for families in crisis, but we can also see how debilitating it can be for a child if they are not taught different dynamics.

- We gave age-appropriate chores and household responsibilities to our daughter, some that only impacted her space, and then gradually ones that impacted the whole family.

- We made it a habit to show gratitude for her follow-through to encourage her capabilities.

3. **Belonging**: When feelings of abandonment and rejection are triggered, a child might question whether they fit and belong in the family.

- One way we saw this play out was with time-outs. I was fond of time-outs with our biological sons because they seemed to work in giving them time to cool down and think about their bad choices. However, these had the opposite effect on our daughter. For her, time-outs triggered feelings of rejection, reinforced separation, and made her feel as though she didn't belong in our family.

- From some reading I did, I discovered the concept of "time-ins." The child needs to sit next to the parent instead of away from them. I tried that a few times, only to see our child's anxiety and stress increase.

- So, I found a solution that worked better in our home. We called these sessions "cool downs." I would sometimes remain in the same room, or close by to encourage safety and communicate that I was with her. I would find some menial tasks to do to pass the time and considered it a cool-down time for me as well. I learned that it didn't matter what we called it, as long as we responded with a method that would reinforce connection and not rejection.

4. **Self-Regulation:** Learning to manage their feelings, emotions, and actions is crucial for many of our children who have experienced trauma.

- We can't expect them to know how, so we must teach them.

- Since there were many instances when our daughter refused to implement what the counselors were teaching her, I worked harder to manage *myself* when I was angry or upset about something because I wanted her to learn healthy techniques for doing so.

- I wanted her to recognize her own value and learn to manage herself; this empowered her to realize that she could grow to be a responsible person.

5. **Self-Awareness:** This quality entails knowledge of one's own character and feelings and how they impact their choices and actions.

- Learning to pay attention to my triggers so I wouldn't respond inappropriately was a learning curve for me, but this became a huge blessing on this parenting journey.

- Because I had learned how to be self-aware in my story, I asked questions that would help our daughter uncover her own understanding of about what she needed and what she needed to change.

- This allowed her to share her heart while giving me deeper insight and understanding of her cognitive abilities and her mental and emotional processing.

6. **Strong Will:** the quality (either positive or negative) of being determined to achieve what one wants.

- We knew from the early days of the adoption that our daughter had a strong will. This didn't intimidate us because we'd had plenty of experience navigating that personality trait with our oldest child. We learned a lot and felt well equipped, all-the-while remembering that a strong-willed individual is different from a person with a strong personality.

- What we didn't know, but quickly learned, is that when *trauma* is part of the narrative, a *strong will* manifests for a different reason. Trauma rewires an individual's brain so that what appears to be clear and predictable might not be. I needed to discern when her strong will was connected to our daughter's personality and when it was a result of her trauma.

- I didn't want to use the trauma as an excuse, but it was clear that it was impacting our daughter's story in many ways. I wanted to help her heal while still holding her accountable for bad choices.

- I found ways to encourage her to use that strong will to do good in her story and not simply push opportunities and people away.

7. **Expectations vs. Consequences:** Making expectations clear for everything, as much as it depended on us, helped us shape our child's heart more effectively.

- When our daughter knew what to expect, she was more apt to respond accordingly.

- Unfortunately, life was going so fast, and there were so many challenges, that sometimes our focus was solely on the consequences.

- We had to revisit our expectations on a regular basis and make sure they were realistic and remained age appropriate.

- Since we had four children in a variety of seasons, we kept in mind their unique abilities as well.

- Consequences need to match the choice the child has made.

- Natural consequences are the most effective.

- Remember that consequences can be positive as well as negative.

8. **Discomfort:** I paid close attention when we were in situations that would or had the potential to make our daughter feel uncomfortable in any way.

- Sometimes I would ask her directly if she was feeling uncomfortable, while other times I would observe the discomfort and speak with her afterward.

- This would help both of us come up with a solution that would help her feel confident and safe.

9. **Anger:** Anger is usually a cover for hurt and pain that can't be articulated or described. To express the underlying emotion in the wrong way can have dire consequences in any relationship.

- I cannot express enough why it is imperative that we uncover the root of our anger. This is one of the emotions that most frequently gets out of hand.

- When anger was expressed verbally or physically, we found that using the following questions helped our daughter to slowly recalibrate: "How can you get what you want in a heathy way?" or "How can I help you get what you need?" instead of "Why are you angry?"

- I reminded myself often that much of the anger was a mask for the deep pain our daughter must have been feeling.

- I spent countless hours in my own personal life addressing, learning to overcome, and getting free from the deep-seated anger I carried in my story. I didn't think I had an anger problem until, as a young mother, I made a list I titled "What makes me angry?" To my shock, within minutes I had sixty-four items written down. Truth be told, only a handful related to anger that might have been justified. Most of them revealed how my loss of control, along with my not getting my way in some situations, impacted me. I had some work to do!

- Once I was able to own the pain in my story, I placed it in the light by verbalizing it and watched it lose its power.

10. **Opinion:** Opinions are a dime a dozen. Everyone has them, and most will freely share them, whether or not they are prompted. Guilty as charged.

- I discovered as our children were learning to articulate their identities through various means that those means weren't always in line with what I thought or felt. Since our family is multiracial, multiethnic, multicultural, and blessed with an adoption, there were lots of opinions available, both from our immediate family members and from others around us.

- Our job as parents was to encourage our children's uniqueness, while encouraging them to anchor their opinions in truth and values they could be proud of.

- Not only did my husband and I differ in our opinions regarding many things, but so did our children.

- To promote harmony in our family after a discussion that was headed in the wrong direction, we decided to coin the clause "That's an opinion thing!" We also used that statement when someone spoke about their preference regarding something simple, such as a food they didn't care for.

- Embracing differences of opinions gave our daughter the freedom to bring her "new" ideas, thoughts, and food choices into our home; this promoted in her a sense of inclusion and belonging.

HOW ABOUT YOU?

What triggers do you carry in your story?

How do you take care of yourself?

What does "belonging" look like to you in your story?

How do the above-mentioned words help you in your personal journey?

14

Ghost Parents

In his book *Adoptees Coming of Age,* Dr. Ron Nydam explains the existence of "ghost parents." Ghost parents are generally the birth parents of the adopted child. Plain and simple. More specifically, the term applies to cases in which the birth parents are not present or involved physically in the life of the child.

The image of birth parents lives deep in the psyche of all children, but with children who have experienced a broken bond from birth parents, their image can sometimes be skewed. However, the children still want to obey them, be loyal to them, and love them in whatever way they know, and they create a picture in their mind's eye of what those absent parents might be or how they might look. In these situations, although the birth parents are *invisible* to us, the child deems them visible in their heart and mind—rendering the term "ghost" parents.

While I journeyed in my understanding of ghost parents, I struggled to some degree. I struggled because, in our daughter's situation, they were often held in higher regard than me.

Our daughter's birth parents *did* exist; they are real people. Her knowledge of them was minimal to nill, so what she believed or fantasized in her mind and heart, though not necessarily reality, was her truth. In her mind her birth mom could do no wrong, was perfect and better to live with than me. In her eyes I was "mean," so there was no way her birth mom could be like me.

That deep desire to be reunited with her birth mom, while restraining her love and loyalty to me, revealed that there might be room in her heart for only her birth parents. I practiced saying, "I cannot and will not compete with her birth parents, as much as it depends on me." I would frequently say this to myself and to anyone else who would listen.

I waited . . . a long time. I learned to acknowledge and surrender those feelings of rejection and those reminders of "not measuring up" that were triggered from my own upbringing. Working at *not* measuring up to an image that existed only in our daughter's mind proved to be just as hard as not working to measure up to someone I could see.

Soon after reading about ghost parents in Dr. Nydam's book, I practiced holding our daughter's birth mother in my mind's eye whenever I interacted with our daughter. For me, this was a tangible reminder that I was not the only mother in her story; I am third. I did not have a picture of that elusive other mother—just a name—so I held it close, reminding me of my position.

Holding the birth mother's name close also helped me with my feelings of fear and anxiety about "getting it wrong." This allowed me to reframe my efforts in a way that highlighted our daughter's unconditional love and acceptance, regardless of this earlier mother's behavior. This was not an easy road, for sure. But in the end, it proved to be extremely rewarding.

As I learned to carry our daughter's birth mother in my heart and mind, it felt as though the two of us mothers were parenting her together. I have no doubt that her mother loved her; after all, she gave her life. I loved her too, and was committed to helping her heal, no matter what.

The *ghost* in "ghost parents" lost its power to threaten my role in our daughter's life. Once I embraced the role her birth mother played in her story, I learned to be grateful for her and see her as a blessing and asset throughout our adoption journey. I share that because I know too many adoptive parents who insist on eradicating every memory of birth parents from the child's narrative. I implore you not to do this, because this approach will rob the child of wholeness and authenticity in their narrative.

I was able to articulate to our daughter what I had learned about ghost parents in the hope that this knowledge would alleviate the growing tension between us. I reminded her that she had three mothers in her story and that perhaps the one *on the scene* (me) was different from the one she deeply desired to be with—the one in her mind. This explanation helped her feel peace, while it gave me confidence to mother her the way I was called to.

HOW ABOUT YOU?

How do "ghost parents" impact your relationship with your adopted child?

What is one issue you need to understand better to parent your adopted child more effectively? In what areas are you trying to measure up to the expectations of others?

15

"Am I Good Enough?"

Recently, as part of my own personal development, I read a book on leadership. In one chapter these three words jumped out at me: *compare*, *compete*, and *climb*. They inspired me to make strong connections to our own story of parenting and empowered me to love our children equally, while treating each uniquely; especially since adoption is part of our narrative.

Compare

Do you compare yourself to other parents? Are you being compared to other parents? Is your child being compared to other children in any way? I suspect that all of us, if we're honest with ourselves, can answer yes to one or more of these questions.

Comparison begins early on, when a parent asks when another parent's child started walking or reached some other milestone. On more than one occasion, I have heard a parent observe, "At least mine isn't as bad as theirs." How hurtful and diminishing. This kind of statement leaves me feeling as though they might compare our situation to theirs behind my back. Maybe you haven't spoken that specific phrase out loud, but the reality is that, whenever a thought enters our mind that pits us against another, we are comparing. What do we gain when comparing our child or approach to parenting with that of another? Absolutely nothing, except maybe a lot of negative results that are useless in terms of serving our child well.

When I first became a mother, I often struggled with the question "Am I good enough?" I knew that I had to unlearn some patterns I had picked up from my own upbringing. As the biological mother of three biracial and multicultural sons, my world was different from that of most of my friends. My husband and I worked hard to help our children celebrate all the cultural nuances we had brought into our family. We knew that we had incorporated different cultures and ethnic backgrounds into our marriage (e.g., "task" vs. "relationship"), but we didn't realize until later on that some of our cultural nuances had been flipped from what would have been the traditional expectation for our culture. For example, as an Indian, my culture tends to be relaxed and unstructured with regard to time. My husband's Dutch culture approaches time in a much more structured manner. However, in our marriage, I was the one who was more structured with time, while my husband's approach to this aspect of life was quite relaxed.

Not only did we want our family to celebrate our respective cultures, but we also needed to help our children understand that we were not a perfect representation of either culture. Every person is a different expression of their culture. Instead of forcing our children to embrace one side or the other, we tried to celebrate all the differences in our home and to watch how those differences manifested in our sons. We came to understand that each of the boys identified with various aspects of both cultures. While we didn't always get it right, we tried to give them the freedom to embrace what they wanted, based at least in part on how they were wired, so they could live and grow into their own narratives in a healthy way. Ironically, in no specific order, one son presents as more American, one as more Indian, and one as more Dutch. Yet all three have a deep appreciation of and respect for each other, for us as parents, and for our stories.

Later, when the opportunity arrived for us to consider adopting our daughter, and as when we journeyed through the adoption process, the question "Am I good enough?" haunted me even more. The idea of comparison showed up again, especially when some people questioned my love for our daughter or suggested that if I "just love[d] her," she would heal. For those who understand the adoption journey, love looks different for each child, and loving requires intentionality that must break through the barrier of trauma and other protective measures the child may have put in place. It wasn't till a few years into our adoption journey that I realized the truth of my having been chosen and called to mother this precious little girl. I learned to accept that I was indeed good enough for her and to identify and respond to her specific needs. It is also true that I didn't realize how much I loved her till I found it necessary to let her go.

HOW ABOUT YOU?

Do you compare your story to someone else's?

What emotions does the question "Am I good enough?" evoke in you? (Feel free to think outside the parenting box.)

Compete

Comparison often leads to competition with another. When we *compete* in our relationships, this almost always leads to dissonance in that relationship, whether it be a marriage, a friendship, or a parent/child association. When I sense that the direction of a conversation has elements of competition in it, I immediately find the need to say, either out loud or in my mind, "I will *not* compete in this relationship!" I desire to place the relationship in the light and not to be tempted to take the path of competition. I remember distinctly that one fellow adoptive parent shared with me that she believed her choice to adopt internationally was beneficial since "those people" wouldn't have access to records and resources in the same way parents of domestically adopted children do. As a non-white, domestic adoptive parent, a mother of four biracial children, and a cultural educator, I was both horrified and strongly tempted to push back and use my knowledge, narrative, and experience to put her in her place. I chose not to do so. I did take the opportunity over the course of a few conversations to learn why she felt that way and how I might educate her with a more positive approach.

As a person who considers herself very competitive, how do I handle the ongoing temptation to compete? I play games in which I can compete to win. Board games, card games, and sports are places where healthy competition belongs. Playing games gives me have a healthy outlet to interact with the relationally competitive people in my life.

In relationships, competing parties run the risk of ensuring that everyone loses.

HOW ABOUT YOU?

Are you competitive? With whom, and in what context?

What do you hope to gain when you compete?

Why do you feel the need to compete?

Climb

Dear friends, we need to learn to *climb* out of those situations that make us feel as though we are not good enough. When I first became a parent, I noticed how many parents would climb onto the shoulders of their children in terms of comparison and competition or simply hide behind the successes of their children. Such parents seem to have forgotten who they are outside their parenting roles; their identity is wrapped up in their title of parent.

Sadly, I was on my way to walking that same path, until one day I had the strong realization that I had gifts, talents, and strengths that were needed outside my world of parenting. Whether in my marriage or my extended family, with friends, or in my community, I embraced the truth that I was and had been "a somebody before, during, and after child rearing." I decided that I would continue to work at nurturing certain qualities in myself in the hope of living as an unapologetic and authentic "me" with my family and those others in my world. I hope that this modeled for our children that they should also be well on their way to living unapologetically and authentically, as themselves.

During my earlier years of parenting, I had a lot of passion (but not necessarily the energy) to serve others. Learning to climb out of the narrow perspective of building a world centered around my children allowed me the ability and energy to help them navigate the world, culture, and era into which they had been born, or—in the case of our daughter—into the world and culture she had joined through adoption. I wanted all of them to learn to serve and to share their gifts and talents with the world. But I couldn't do that if I walked the path of enabling them, encouraging entitlement, or refusing opportunities to serve that came my way.

In their adult years, two of our sons lived in a state with a majestic mountain range that invited them into the world of hiking and mountain climbing. During our many visits, I didn't participate on those hikes or climbs due to some of my physical challenges. My husband, on the other hand, was always eager and ready to join them. Hearing about their adventures on their hikes and climbs reminded me of our journey through parenting and adoption. Lots of climbing was happening. It took some very difficult conversations for me to realize that we were both skilled and equipped—though differently. My husband had the ability to manage physical challenges and to negotiate the physical and practical valley experiences we needed to climb out of, while I was equipped to handle the mental and emotional challenges and valleys. Together we were stronger for the climb.

HOW ABOUT YOU?

What valley do you need to climb out of? Or what mountain might you be ready or equipped to climb?

What tools or support do you need in your climb based on the challenges you are equipped to face? (For example, practical/ physical or mental/emotional challenges.)

Who in your circle is equipped to help with your climb?

16

Parenting Is a Marathon

Let me say at the beginning of this chapter that some of my suggestions regarding rest and respite are based on our unique story and won't necessarily work for everyone. I completely understand that finding rest and respite will not look the same for every parent and, in some cases, won't be experienced on a regular basis. Based on your narrative, however, I encourage you to consider how my story can empower you. There are questions at the end of this chapter inviting you to consider any changes you may want or need to make in the hope that you will be better equipped for this marathon of parenting. Not a parent? You can still answer many of the questions and even find ways to provide support and encouragement for someone else who is.

If I am completely honest, and at the risk of sounding as though I am bragging, please know that I don't mean to. It's just that, for me, being self-aware, taking care of myself, and guarding my boundaries have always come easily. But somewhere along the journey of parenting four children, two of whom confronted us with significant challenges, I was still fraying emotionally. I felt as though I were swimming in an ocean with no shore to swim toward. How did that happen?

It appeared that I was on the brink of burnout and needed *major* respite. With the blessing of my husband, I took three days away from my daily responsibilities and expectations. I arranged activities that sang to my soul and anticipated a lot of fun. I arranged for our daughter to stay at the home of a *trusted* friend. I needed to know that she was with a friend who would be consistent with the guidelines we had in place regarding dealing with her trauma. I didn't want her and me to return home, only to face more trauma triggers because of our time apart from each other. Sometimes we can help minimize our child's triggers and curb their negative behaviors by being *thoughtful* about what environments they are in. Frankly, even though some people offered to help, their lack of understanding about the specific needs of our family caused them to be part of the problem rather than the solution.

As I was processing aloud with a friend of mine the things I had learned from this intentional time away, I understood my state of mind in the form of an analogy. I described it like this: my situation was like Superman next to Kryptonite. His energy was depleted, his strength sapped, and he was losing control of his body; his circumstances were sucking the life out of him. My situation felt the very same way. I am not Superwoman, as some have called me, but the day-in and day-out work required of me to stay intentionally engaged took a toll on me mentally, emotionally, and spiritually and eventually showed up physically. The day-to-day challenge of this child's need for control, her defiance, the lying, the manipulation, and the needs of our other children together felt like Kryptonite. I was losing the ability to care for myself in the usual ways that had always sustained me and brought me great joy.

Just about every aspect of my parenting seemed focused on stealing, killing, and destroying all that was good in me. To top it off, the expectations of friends, family, and others in our community added to my exhaustion. This was affecting our marriage and many other things I was passionate about. I know that I was on the brink of burnout, but I couldn't even find my voice to express it.

I love all our children equally and feel blessed to be a parent. However, as you may well know, parenting can come with a lot of challenges and simply be exhausting! When one or more children are dealing with trauma or other personal challenges or disabilities in their narrative, our responsibilities are multi-layered, . . . and so are our emotions. We not only need to address their physical, nutritional, mental, emotional, spiritual, and social needs, but we must find the strength and time to do the same for ourselves. Somewhere along the way, I think we believe that *all* the needs of our children are *fully* our responsibility. Key word "fully." Here is a news flash that may be welcome to you: they are *not!* Let me clarify. The child *is* our responsibility, but sometimes we need help from others to carry out that responsibility. Parents, we can't pour out to our children what we don't have inside us. When we try to do that, we exhaust our stamina and don't have sufficient reserve for the *marathon* of parenting.

My question to you is this: How do you take care of yourself physically, mentally, emotionally, nutritionally, or spiritually? Sometimes this requires that we change some of our own behaviors to prioritize caring for ourselves. At other times, the child(ren) may need to learn by trying or by helping to carry a specific responsibility that is appropriate for them to do. Or you may need to ask for outside help. When was the last time you reached out to your spouse, partner, family members, pastor, friends, counselors, teachers, coaches, or doctors, and asked them for help to carry the load? Help didn't always come in the form we expected or wanted, but at least I learned to ask for it.

Here's an analogy that supports the need for self-care. Traveling is one of my many passions, and a plane is my favorite mode of transportation. Prior to take-off, the flight attendant addresses the passengers and crew over the loudspeaker, in part on how to prepare for a potential emergency. When the attendant gives instructions about how and when to apply the oxygen mask, they instruct you to put the mask *securely* on yourself *first* and then on your child next to you. That's how we need to approach parenting; this is even more critical when you are dealing with a traumatized child. Do what you need to do to catch your own breath, organize your priorities, and seek help; you'll be better equipped for the journey ahead.

Don't listen to anyone who claims that their way is the only right way when it comes to rest, respite, or self-care. Just as with the mask analogy, the flight attendant asks us to "pull the strings till the mask fits over *your* face." The same is true with regard to this concept of rest: find a way that works for your family and your narrative. You might even have to *tighten* your purse strings in some situations to financially afford the rest you need.

All right, parents, let's don the "mask," take a deep breath, and take off on this marathon together!

Here are some questions that might help you address areas in which you need rest or get a better handle on your priorities. Along the way, be sure to celebrate the small wins!

Physically:

What does physical activity look like in your story? In a typical day or week?

What gets in the way of your getting physically active?

How much quality sleep are you getting? Or are you having trouble sleeping?

Mentally:

How do you handle chaos or stress?

What do you believe about your body? (Note: Our thoughts directly affect our physical wellbeing and care.)

How much mental rest are you getting?

What do you do to relax?

Do you struggle with mental illness? Are you getting help?

What does thought management look like in your story?

Emotionally:

How truthful are you about your feelings?

Practice filling in the blanks of this statement for different scenarios: "When ____happens, I feel____." (Remember that feelings are not right or wrong—they just are.)

How do you handle your own triggers?

How do you cope with grief and loss?

What does emotional health mean to you? And how are you growing it in your story?

Nutritionally:

How do you view food (e.g., necessity or privilege)?

How do you decide what to snack on?

What place does food have in your story?

Do you have challenges with food (e.g., eating disorder, allergies, lack of resources or access)?

Socially:

Are you taking time to connect with friends? Why or why not?

Are friends taking time to connect with you? How are you responding?

What does your social circle look like? Do you feel supported by others?

Can you name those who speak life into you?

Are you surrounded by any toxic relationships?

When was the last time you thanked a friend for being just that—a friend?

What role do your friends play in the life of your child?

Change comes slowly—be sure to move ahead at your pace, and please don't be hard on yourself. Ask for help where you need it. Not sure where that is? If you haven't already done so, I encourage you to seek out a trusted friend or mentor to help you navigate this marathon of parenting. Don't go it alone. We are stronger when we go the distance together!

HOW ABOUT YOU?

What will you do to address self-care in your story?

17

Marriage Matters

[Note: When I speak of marriage, I am referring to our heterosexual marriage because that is the foundation of our story. I am making general comments in relation to how marriages are impacted by unique adjustments that need to be made when parenting an adopted child. Many of these children carry needs left behind from their trauma of relinquishment. Each relationship will be different, but these deficits/needs could present in similar ways. This may not be your reality, but I hope that this chapter will still have a positive impact on your relationship.]

If you are a married parent or in a long-term relationship (functioning as marriage) and responsible for children, you understand that marriage matters and that there are unique issues in relation to marriage: time, unity, oneness, and finances, just to name a few of the many matters that challenge us in our roles as parents. In the case of parenting the adopted child, the statistics are extremely high with regard to marriages ending in separation or divorce because of the challenges this kind of relationship exposes.

Let's start by listening to what I might have told my younger self about marriage:

You don't know what you are getting into.

Don't expect that it will be all fun and games.

God uses marriage to make you holy, not necessarily happy.

Be open to change.

Don't take yourself so seriously.

Learn to keep saying "I do" to your spouse.

Keep pursuing your spouse or partner.

Do your personal heart work.

Find time to laugh together.

Learn to laugh at yourself.

Be a student of your spouse.

For years, my husband and I thought we were doing all the right things in our marriage and felt that our becoming parents of strong-willed children was the center of our stress. We went to a marriage counselor for a season early in our marriage, I got personal counseling throughout those years, we had experienced mentors to speak into our relationship, and we attended marriage conferences and did the work we were asked to do.

Then it happened . . .

We eventually sought a family counselor for the extreme challenges we were facing with our then sixteen-year-old. To our surprise, the counselor stated, "You don't have a parenting problem; you have a marriage problem!"

We were both quite shocked at that statement because we were not seeing it. By that I mean that we thought we had a great marriage, although we both acknowledged that it required working hard. Because of the struggles we were facing with our teenager, we thought the issue had to be a parenting problem.

The reality hit when the counselor looked at my husband and made a statement my heart and words had failed to articulate in our marriage: "Your wife is hard-wired for unity." He explained in so many words that all my efforts were focused on attempts to keep us all connected . . . and that my husband was undermining them. Queue my tears.

I had waited for someone to get through to Ken, and finally it happened. The counselor *had seen* me and really *heard* me. I was not angry at my husband for any of that, although his lack of follow-through with the kids had been frustrating from time to time. But I was hopeful that this would be a turning point. It was.

From that day forward, my husband began getting involved with the heavy lifting in parenting. As a teammate. Our son continued along his strong-willed path, and we all came out of the situation with relational battle scars, but we together journeyed the road to deep healing several months later.

Because we are also adoptive parents, I thought it important for you to hear what I was told by other adoptive parents regarding the impact adoption has had on their marriages. Many of their comments resonated with me . . . and broke my heart yet again. If any of their remarks resonate with you, please know that you are not alone in your struggle. Please reach out and get the help you all need.

I asked the following question on my social media site: "How has adoption impacted your marriage?" These were some of the responses I received:

- I carry more of the load (mother).

- Sometimes I regret adopting our child because of how much his story is affecting our family.

- We are always so exhausted from the rage episodes and the countless doctor/therapist appointments.

- We struggle with intimacy, both emotionally and sexually.

- My wife does not take me seriously when I suggest we need outside help.

- My husband does not take me seriously when I suggest we need help.

- I am not emotionally available. He is not physically available.

- I hate feeling so triggered so much of the time.

- I don't like feeling so angry.

- Why can't my spouse be more involved?

- We used to have so much fun together as a couple before we adopted.

- I don't feel emotionally and intellectually stimulated by my spouse.

We believe that the family foundation finds its strength in the unity of the parents. No parents are perfect, and no marriage is perfect because it's made up of imperfect people. As parents, we have the responsibility to strengthen our marriages so that our children experience safety and a deep sense of belonging as they grow up.

How would you rate the strength of your relationship? What might you do differently to strengthen it? I am not questioning your commitment to your spouse/partner, and I am not being judgmental of your differing opinions of what constitutes the foundation of a family. I am simply asking you to consider where your marriage/partnership is at, because marriage matters are constantly changing.

Want to improve your marriage and address the matters that are affecting you personally?

Below are forty-five questions I came up with—you can add your own along the way—that will help build a dialogue with your spouse in the hope that your connection will get stronger and that, over time, you will be able to address the marriage matters in your relationship.

This list of questions has been used in our marriage and asked of a variety of couples in different seasons of relationship. Some questions are faith-based because that helped us immensely, while others have a different focus. We encourage you to get creative and share these questions with your spouse/partner in a way that might strengthen your marriage or partner relationship and help move you closer to one another in small and yet significant ways.

1. Is accountability in the marriage or committed partnership needed? Not needed? Benefits? What does this look like in your relationship?

2. In what ways do you maintain healthy competition in your relationship? Are there games and activities that contribute to that?

3. How have you seen God answer prayer in your story lately— both individually and in your relationship?

4. What does intimacy mean to you?

5. Is it sex? If so, how is that area of your relationship going? If the two of you aren't on the same page in this regard, what needs to change?

6. What topic is the most difficult for you to talk to your spouse or partner about? Why?

7. In what ways—that worked—did you pursue your spouse this week?

8. Whose voice is louder in your ear than your spouse's or partner's? Whose opinion matters more than theirs? Would your spouse or partner agree with, or be surprised by, the name you shared?

9. What activity do you trust your spouse to engage in without your "supervision"? Why?

10. Name something very important to you that you don't think your spouse understands, views the same away, or can relate to.

11. In what ways do you "need" your spouse?

12. In what areas of your marriage could you include your spouse more?

13. In friendships/relationships/marriage, what is more important to you?

    a) frequency of time together

    b) quality (depth and connection)

    c) both

14. What are some key values you want to see grow in your marriage? What do you hope to see in this regard when you look back x number of years from now?

15. "Who's the boss in your marriage?

16. A What insecurities does your spouse have that you are aware of? What insecurities do you have that negatively impact your relationship?

17. In what area(s) do you find yourself making excuses for your spouse? Why do you suspect this is?

18. Is there an "if . . . then" or a "because . . . therefore" clause operative from either or both directions in your marriage vows? (When there is a "therefore," we must ask what it is there for!) *Love* is a verb that needs to be lived out in action.

19. What in your marriage makes you feel disrespected or not heard or validated?

20. On a scale of 1–10 (with 1 being low), how much do you *enjoy* your spouse (not just sexually)? What will it take to move this number upward?

21. With regard to yourself, what is your spouse's favorite body part (unless you can rate a top 5!)?

22. Name a pet peeve you have with regard to your spouse. How do you handle the situation when this comes into play?

23. How valuable do you see yourself in your marriage?

24. Share a comment or two about you from the mouth of your spouse that sounds negative to you. Discuss.

25. How does your *desire* for your spouse or partner impact your *identity* and cause you to *act* in ways that either help you grow forward together or add struggles to your relationship?

26. How, if at all, does the declaration "I want what God wants for my marriage" play out in your story? Where and how does this show up?

27. What does vulnerability look like in your marriage?

28. How do you handle cultural differences in your marriage (culture = family, ethnicity, nationality, work, etc.)?

29. If you believe that "silence is implicit," in what area(s) are you remaining silent in your marriage when you should speak out? In what context should you be silent and not speak? (This applies to all relationships, not just within the marriage or with regard to race/culture differences.)

30. In what ways does your marriage relationship challenge your boundaries?

31. How and where do your "love languages" show up in your relationship? (*The Five Love Languages*: words of affirmation, quality time, receiving gifts, acts of service, and physical touch).

32. What stands in the way of your truly expressing yourself to your spouse or partner?

33. What does it look like for your spouse or partner to demonstrate that they have your back (e.g., "I've got your six")?

34. Share something new that you learned about your spouse or partner recently.

35. How do you as an individual cultivate intimacy with God?

36. How do your apologies impact your actions going forward? Does your spouse or partner notice and affirm your attempts to back them up? How does their response affect you?

37. What situations, circumstances, or people cause you to separate and move away from each other or repel you from each other?

38. How do you anticipate the needs of your spouse or partner? When was the last time you did so?

39. What do you see when you look into your spouse's or partner's eyes? Go ahead and tell them.

40. What does flirting with your spouse or partner look like in your relationship? What results is this having?

41. How does mutual submission show up in your relationship with your spouse or partner?

42. Do you "water" seeds of hope or doubt in your marriage?

43. What does surrender (letting go) look like in your relationship? How do you behave when you don't get your way?

44. When was the last time you did something for your spouse or partner without expecting anything in return?

45. In what areas are you being a "student of your spouse"? Where do you need to do better at learning about them as they grow?

46. Share why you said "I do" in the first place (married couples). Share why you stay committed to each other (unmarried but together).

Note: I encourage you to repeat #45 as often as possible because parenting can easily make us forget our primary commitment to one another. Doing so also affords new life and strength to the relationship.

18

Vision of a War Horse

A few years after the adoption was final, I began to realize that the struggle of loss and trauma from relinquishment and adoption was real. The challenges became more frequent, frustrations were increasing on both sides, and everything just seemed arduous.

Around that time, we watched the movie *War Horse*. The movie is based on the journey of a black stallion during a civil war. He was stolen from the "good guys" by the "bad guys." In a particular scene, the horse finds and takes the opportunity to escape back to his previous owners. But while the horse is escaping, he gets tangled up in three consecutive barbed wire fences and collapses in the middle of no-man's land. He struggles to free himself, to no avail. The more he fights, the harder the barbed wire pierces his muscular body.

Finally, a soldier from the "good" side waves a white flag of peace so he can safely and freely go onto the battlefield to rescue the horse. During his first attempt, he is threatened by shots fired from behind enemy lines. His second attempt to reach the horse is successful. Ironically, a soldier from behind enemy lines comes to help with wire cutters in his hands. He has knowledge and a resource. He wants to share that knowledge, so the cutting of the wires and the freeing of the horse are done in such a way that neither the horse nor anyone else is hurt. For the moment while the rescue is the focus, both soldiers are on the same team, wanting the same outcome.

So, you may ask, what does this have to do with parenting the adopted child? The other day I was reminded of this visual when our daughter was in one of her dark times.

I saw her as the stallion with the barbed wire of her story wrapped around her, piercing her struggling body. She was trying to free herself from her own challenges, while her tenacity and strong will were only causing her more pain. I felt helpless. Many of you parents have been in similar situations, so you know what I am talking about.

Over the years, I too have asked for help. I have waved my white flag. But unfortunately, I did not always get the help I needed. In some cases, I had to force myself to be grateful even though the "help" we were given was causing more challenges. I learned to receive intended help in any form because it allowed space to consider what did and didn't work in our situation. I knew I had a lot to learn, so I didn't lose hope. I often live by the motto "If at first you don't succeed, try, try again." I did. I tried again to get help. I believe God provided in those situations.

Through counseling, a new school, and a staff of teachers and administrators who understood the various aspects of our adoption journey, we were often given the help we needed along the way. Yet a question was always at the forefront of my mind: "Will I cooperate with the help I am receiving?"

Let's go back to the movie clip. One of the soldiers came to the scene with wire cutters to help free the horse. He worked together with his enemy, the soldier from the other side, to get the job done in an efficient way for the sake of the horse. They put their differences aside for the moment and did what was in the best interest of the stallion. The result was that their revised mission was accomplished. The horse was freed! I believe this applies well for us as parents and other involved parties who long to be united in our efforts for the sake of the children. The best we can do is stand together, set aside differences, and focus on finding the best solution for the wellbeing of the child. Sadly, too many parents respond to challenging situations through the lens of their own unresolved issues based on their own narratives that are peppered with trauma, stress, or selfish desires.

Although it was challenging at times, we did everything we could to cooperate with each other and with our "helpers" during that season. We didn't always agree with their methods—or each other's, for that matter—but we attempted to trust in their expertise and then modified their suggestions to fit our narrative, beliefs, and value system. We knew our child needed help, but the responsibility was ours to set the example of seeking the help and cooperating to achieve a positive outcome for all parties involved.

HOW ABOUT YOU?

Are you on the same side as your child?

Who are the people and tools in your story who are beneficial in helping your child break free from the "barbed wires" in their story?

How do you handle challenges in your story?

Are you an individual who is still feeling the effects of the pain and "piercings" in your own story?

19

Knowing Your Strength

"How do you get what you want in a healthy way?" is a question I have asked myself personally on many occasions as I worked on my control issues. Asking this question proved to be instrumental in my parenting as well, especially with our strong-willed children. It taught me to tone down my attitude and my need for control without diminishing my strengths. By using this question, I could still have my needs met, but in ways that showed greater respect and kindness, while not coming off as demanding. This may be an elementary method to you, but this simple question gave me a tangible tool to disarm a negative trait I had carried in my story for far too long.

So, how do you get what *you* want in a healthy way?

There were countless moments in our parenting journey when we had to ask this question. It started with me. I had to find new and healthy approaches to achieving results before I could expect my children to follow suit.

I learned that the roots of my emotional unhealthiness stemmed from unresolved pain from a variety of sources and relationships. I needed to stop using anger as my go-to emotion when giving commands or instructions or asking for obedience. It took a minute—okay, a few years of counseling, processing out loud, journaling, confessing, forgiving, and apologizing—to finally get to the root of the problem and learn new patterns. We are all on a journey, right?

That strength I had was indeed toxic, and I had some work to do. Here is a written excerpt from my first book, *I Am Hagar: Forgotten No More*, in which I unpack my personal learning and the tools I used:

While reading the book The High Cost of High Control *by Dr. Tim Kimmel, I discovered that the strength I had was actually "toxic strength" and that it would need to be turned into a strength that was more useful and reveal more of how and what I was created for.*

Shortly thereafter, my husband recommended another book called NOW: Discovering Your Strengths *by Marcus Buckingham and Donald O. Clifton, PhD.*

This second book challenged me to take the Clifton Strengths test that would help me gain a deeper understanding of the strengths I did have and put words to them. After answering several questions that would eventually "diagnose" my strengths, I was given these top five:

Connectedness, Responsibility, Activator, Belief and Winning-Others-Over *(for those who like acronyms as I do, CRAB-WOO). Just by themselves, they are a great list of strengths that helped me develop in confidence, not only in my business but in parenting and my marriage as well. It didn't take long before I was aware of the strengths that were of the toxic nature. Responsibility and Activator. Strengths are good for us to have. But they also have a hidden side that could cause us to develop a hard heart or grow a belief that "we don't need others; we are strong enough by ourselves." **I've learned (through several situations-gone-bad) that the best results come when we can acknowledge our weaknesses amid those strengths.***

After taking the Clifton Strengths test and finding out that my strength of responsibility caused me to drift into feeling overly responsible for some people and situations, I came up with a reminder tool to help me stay on track. I call it my "2 x 4 Rule." This was transformational for me not only in parenting our children but also in my marriage and with my clients. In my parenting, this tool allows me to achieve what I want in a healthy way and my children and husband to shine in their own strengths. While I'm with my clients, it allows me to keep a healthy emotional distance.

So, what is the 2 x 4 Rule? It's simply learning when to be responsible *to* (2) someone rather than *for* (4) them. As parents of young children, we recognize that we are fully responsible for them and for their physical and emotional needs. But as the children get older, we need to allow them to be responsible for the age-appropriate behaviors they are capable of, taking into consideration any physical or emotional disabilities they may have. Over time and with their growing maturity, we need to move from being responsible *for* them to becoming responsible *to* them—ensuring, of course, that they have the resources they need to carry out their responsibility on their own. When we choose to *do* everything for a child, we potentially debilitate them from the autonomy they were created to have as a unique and maturing individual.

In the early years of parenting, I noticed that my stress would build when I tried to get our oldest son to do his homework. I imagine that many of you parents are standing with me in that stress!! But I believed (and was told by other mothers) that "good mothers make sure their children do their homework."

Our family counselor helped me realize that my job as the parent was to provide the necessary supplies that the child needed, a conducive working environment, and the required time they needed to complete the work they were assigned to do. But it was not my responsibility to ensure that they completed the homework, and it was certainly not my responsibility to do the homework for them. That was a game changer for me—and for the climate in our home.

This different perspective gave me an opportunity to shift the responsibility from myself to the school-aged child. I had been feeling and taking on more of the responsibility when it was not mine to carry. This allowed me to allow the teacher to hold our children accountable. As I learned to be more responsible *to* our children by making sure they had what they needed for their assignments, I started to feel calmer. The power struggle over homework vanished. It was now their responsibility to do the homework . . . or not. I was *not* responsible *for* the homework itself or for the outcome. The consequences were all theirs. I did, however, apply consequences with regard to the boundaries in our home. For example, the following conversation often occurred in one iteration or another:

Child: "Can I watch my show?"

Me: "Absolutely, feel free to watch that show you want . . . when your homework is done."

Child: "But I don't want to do my homework."

Me: "Bummer. I guess you really don't want to watch your show either then. Because the show comes on only when the homework is done."

Child: (no comment)

Applying my 2 x 4 Rule resulted in the children learning accountability while the responsibility and pressure were removed from me and put onto the school and the teachers who had assigned the homework. This allowed for some restoration in my relationship with the children. The counselor challenged me to think of it this way: "Kinita, you didn't assign the homework, so why are you holding yourself responsible for it?" This perspective made for an interesting learning curve for all of us, but it had great applications in many areas.

I implemented my 2 x 4 Rule with chores as well. Growing up, I hated to do chores, and our children were no different. Managing a family of four children was a lot of work, to say the least, so we developed a chore chart that we used over the course of several years. Each week a child would be assigned different age-appropriate chores so they could have a variety of experiences. (Future spouses or partners, you can thank me later—but I digress).

For one of our children, setting the table for dinner seemed too often to be forgotten when it was their week to do so. This gave us a great opportunity to practice the 2 x 4 Rule and "shift responsibility" in this area. One evening, the table did not get set . . . *again!* So, we all sat down, with the pots of food in the middle of the table. It was obvious that there were no plates or silverware. Before you prejudge what I am about to share, I want to remind you that you were not there. I was tired of this child not following through with his responsibilities, so I did the first thing that came to my mind. I served the food right on the table! That got his attention! He immediately jumped up and got plates. And he never forgot again.

We unpacked the situation afterward, only to discover that because he hated to do any of his chores, he simply put the responsibility out of his mind. Together we came up with a plan. When it was his week to set the table, we agreed that he would ask me approximately what time dinner was scheduled to be served. He would then write a note or set the timer to remind himself to perform this task five to ten minutes before dinner would be ready. Desperate times call for desperate measures! I am just thankful we were not having curry that night.

The lesson here is that, when I applied the 2 x 4 Rule, I was responsible *to* the family by making the meal and making sure everyone understood the expectations with regard to the chores chart. And the incident reinforced to our son that he was responsible *for* setting the table.

When our daughter joined our family, a deeper layer of control was revealed in me. I don't think I am alone in this. Since we had adopted her I believed there was always something I could do to help heal her from her emotional pain. But being responsible *for* her emotional pain wasn't mine to own—or so I thought. I was only partly right. Her life experience before joining our family was not my responsibility. But what happened afterward exposed how I would have to rethink my approach in many situations.

One final example: the schoolwork struggle showed up in our daughter, yet for different reasons than for her brothers. I would sometimes sit with the children and help them navigate their homework or listen to them read, but I noticed that our daughter's anxiety increased if I sat next to her during her homework time. I tried a variety of ways to maintain the pattern *I wanted*, thinking that the issue was as simple as her not being accustomed to parental supervision or support. But instead, I noticed that *my presence was causing more challenges for both of us*. Her screaming and my demanding, which included some unrealistic expectations, wasn't working for either of us. It wasn't helping the other children, either, as they were trying to concentrate on their homework. Not my best moments, for sure. I wanted the best for her, but, clearly, I was not going about it the right way.

I came up with a solution I didn't love, but it helped her at least a little. I changed my timing of dinner preparations to while she was sitting at the dining table doing her homework. This way I was still within earshot of her reading. This adjustment was needed so that, when we attended parent/teacher conferences, I could give honest feedback about her progress and her struggles. It also allowed me to be available to answer any questions she might have, in conjunction with the bonus of my ability to take care of my responsibility *to* my family by making dinner.

Being responsible *to* and *for* really does look different in various relationships. But in the end, it is important to harness our need for control, while enhancing the other person's need for autonomy.

HOW ABOUT YOU?

In what areas do you struggle with control?

How do your strengths impact your parenting?

How do you go about getting what you want?

How does not getting your way make you feel?

20

Being Steadfast

Steadfast is an older word that isn't commonly used these days. It does, however, seem to be common to some, but not all, faith communities.

The dictionary defines steadfast as "fixed in direction, place and position; firm in purpose; resolution, faith, attachment, unwavering adherence; firmly established."

I thought it was interesting that the dictionary defined the word in part as "attachment." If you are an adoptive parent, the significance isn't lost on you. Our adopted kiddos often struggle with attachment because the first parental bond was broken in their story. We as adoptive parents work hard to help them attach. As a mother, I worked hard to get our daughter to attach, sometimes too hard. From counseling appointments to medication and behavioral therapy, I kept trying to find ways to help her attach better—not always with success. This can be an exhausting season of life when we are so intentional about the work.

At the end of the day, I am not convinced that there is anything we can proactively do to affect the attachment of the child's heart. Don't get me wrong—that doesn't mean we don't try. It does mean that we can't control/force the child into a place of attachment. They have to *want* to go there. And we need to provide an environment that makes them feel as though they can. That is not always an easy task.

But there's hope. We, from our side, can attach. We can be consistent. We can follow through. We can be truthful about our feelings, hang in there, and learn to be present. I'll be honest: it was very difficult for me to want to stay attached to a child I believed didn't wanted to choose me. She longed for her birth mother and feared losing memory of her if she didn't get her back. That kind of rejection from the child is painful on a good day and torturous on a bad one. Day in and day out, rejection, rejection, rejection. How does one attach to someone they believe doesn't want them?

This kind of relationship can also have toxic qualities. I am not a stranger to toxic relationships and have had to work hard to remain healthy in the midst of them. So, what hope do we have of experiencing healthy parent/child relationships when one or both people are toxic?

First, make sure you are not the toxic one. Second, do your part. Stay grounded, stand on the foundation of why you felt called to become an adoptive parent in the first place, lean into your faith (whatever it may be), grow in self-awareness, take care of yourself, and maintain healthy boundaries (more about this later). You don't have to be a Christian to be able to do these things, but in my experience the power God gives me to be patient and long-suffering in this parenting journey certainly grows the peace I need in my heart.

This looks good on paper, but it is hard to experience relief if your foundation for parenting is not secure and grounded. If that is true in your story, it is time to take back your life and start making changes. Growth will happen only if you are willing to do the hard work.

Recently, as I was unpacking this idea with a trusted friend of mine, we used an analogy that might help clarify what I am trying to say to you. A rebar is a steel rod used to strengthen concrete and hold concrete together. For the child carrying trauma in their story, there is often a deep need for control that eventually births a strong will, which is often misused. When she doesn't get her way, our daughter digs in her heels and appears to be immovable. Wielding this need for control, a child is actually protecting herself in an unhealthy way. Then comes defiance. And on and on it goes. It becomes a vicious cycle of control, strong will, and defiance. This cycle actually reinforces the old patterns in her heart and mind, in the same way a rebar does. Clearly not helpful!

However, we the parents can also develop the "rebar" strength in a positive way: by being stable, firm, supportive, and immovable— grounded in a healthy way.

Our kiddos need us to possess an unwavering strength. They need to know that we won't keel over when they push into us. They need to know that their pain is not stronger or bigger than our resources. We need to show them resilience and a hang-in-there attitude, so as not to inadvertently reinforce what they might have experienced in their first families. By the way, this also applies to parenting biological children. Can you do that?

What do you need to do differently today to show your child that you are going to stay upright and not fall over when they push into you? For me, it started with an apology and asking my child to help me. This allowed her to feel useful in my story.

I don't know about you or your story—I only know mine. I don't always have the strength in myself to withstand the rejection my children throw at me. It can feel pretty major sometimes. That's why I lean into my faith even more. It informs me with exactly what I need in the moment and for the days following. I have assimilated the truth of the phrase "Many hands make light work." I choose to see God as the Hand that helps me carry this challenge, burden, and responsibility, so that the work of parenting a child who can't or doesn't want to attach becomes somehow lighter.

HOW ABOUT YOU?

In what area(s) do you need to practice being more steadfast?

Do you struggle with attachment? If so, how?

What does consistency look like in your story?

21

"I Need You to Wait"

The window of time between the afterschool hours and dinner was often an extremely stressful time in our home, as four children arrived home from school, often tired, hungry, and grumpy. As much as I tried to maintain routine and order in our home during this time, the challenging emotions, moods, and behaviors would continuously push on my boundaries.

This day was no different. Our daughter came home from school and appeared to have hit yet another emotional wall. This one seemed different from the one she had faced that morning before going to school. I had a strong sense that something else was going on. It wasn't a "strong-will-get-my-way" kind of day. I didn't know it at the time, but the expectations she faced at school with relationships, on top of the regular challenges of academics, were pushing her to her limit.

To avoid overreacting, I did the usual by encouraging her to implement her cool-down and self-regulating strategies. She responded with defiance and attitude again and again. This was not just her strong will speaking. It was her trauma. Although I had neither the language to respond nor a specific understanding of the issues at the moment, I began to recognize this dynamic more and more often as time went on.

Because I was so caught up with my schedule of getting the dinner of enchiladas and homemade guacamole ready to put on the table, piping hot at just the right time, I didn't have the time or the patience to meet her in a space where she needed me the most. I regret that. I regret not knowing what to do and not taking the time then to meet her in that space. Instead, I unintentionally added to her pain.

Despite the pain and suffering she was experiencing, I needed something: I needed her to wait. I needed her to wait so I could provide a proper meal for my family. I needed her to respect me and my time. I needed her to meet *my* needs in this small way. I suspect that you are thinking I was being selfish and inconsiderate, failing to meet the immediate needs of my child. You are right.

You know why? I was exhausted and felt as though I wasn't doing a good job of mothering. I also thought that trying to raise this daughter was killing me on the inside and that, at that moment, the only thing I felt I could do with any success was cook a meal. Yes, I had needs, and I was trying to find a way to get them met, even while I felt I was failing at everything else.

With a firm, yet soft voice, I asked her to wait and reassured her I would make time for her after I had finished preparing dinner. I also asked her to repeat the statement "I need to wait" out loud, while she waited. This was all I could think of in that moment—to give her an opportunity to connect words to a related action. She repeated the statement three or four times. And then the tears began to flow from those big brown eyes, and a peace came over her. It wasn't a give-up-and-give-in-to-mom resignation but a peaceful and relieved kind of calm. I had learned the difference.

After I successfully got dinner in the oven, I sat down with her and her communication journal and began our usual check-in. The check-in was a consistent method I used with her to give us both the opportunity to ask questions and to help me listen to what she was—and wasn't—saying.

Even though she appeared to hate check-ins and these routine conversations, and on many occasions told me so, I felt as though I had to do something to help us connect, to help her heal, and to help both of us figure out how to navigate this relationship. I just made every attempt to allow time for these check-ins when both of us were in good headspace.

That's when I discovered her true needs. On this afternoon, my interaction with my daughter reminded me once again of the Bible story of Rachel and Leah to which I've referred more than once. As the story goes, Leah had to wait her turn because Rachel was the one who was chosen. I have frequently used this story, this example of a need for waiting, as a strong analogy in my own journey. On that particular afternoon, I heard very clearly: "Kinita, you need to wait your turn."

After the events of that afternoon, I did some reflecting and decided that I needed to write down some ways in which I would learn to wait. Here are some points I wrote down:

- I need to wait my turn. I am reminded again that "I am third."

- I need to wait to tell her certain pieces of her story. She doesn't want to or isn't ready to hear them yet.

- I need to wait to step into her space of girlhood. She hasn't invited me into that space yet.

- I need to wait and lean into my faith so that I can be my best self; then, when she does invite me in, I can effectively help in the shaping of her heart.

- I need to wait for her to accept me as her mother. She hasn't done that, and I need to be okay with that, . . . even if she never accepts me.

- I need to wait for someone to walk with me on this lonely path of parenting.

On some days, to be totally honest, I was tired of waiting. I just wanted to cry. On those days my journal pages filled up quickly with ponderings on this painful reality. My prayers for our daughter were deep and filled with anguish over the trauma and heartache she carried around in her heart. My pillowcase was often stained with my tears before I fell asleep. Often, those tears flowed when I heard a song on the radio that reminded me of God's unconditional love for me and how I needed to pour that same unconditional love out to her. I really do want to pour out that kind of love to her. I just need to wait for her to receive it.

Through this situation, and many similar occasions, I learned how to "be" more rather than to "do" more. I learned to be present, . . . while waiting. I was reminded again and again that our daughter really did need *me*. Her choices and actions cried this out. I needed to show her love in the language she understood and not in the ways I thought would work. But I would first need to wait for her to invite me into those spaces.

HOW ABOUT YOU?

What do you need to change so that you can learn to *wait* rather than always *do*?

In what ways do you identify with me as a parent or with our daughter?

What are you doing to evaluate your role as a parent?

22

What Do You Need?

"What do you need?" Such a great question for someone to ask, . . . and yet, sadly, one that was not asked of us as often as I needed. I love that question because it not only shows concern on the part of the person who is asking, but it allows the person being asked the question to feel seen. It also allows us parents a chance to pause and consider what we do need in the season we are in. Unfortunately, for us as parents in the thick of challenges and situations beyond our control, we often feel as though we are drowning and might not have the capacity to share what we really need. That was true for us on many occasions.

Although I have always been comfortable with asking for help, in the times when I felt as though I was drowning, asking for help seemed pointless. I felt as though the person from whom I was seeking help wanted me to *undrown* myself before they could understand and empathize with my needs. My blank stare and confused expression usually showed them that I was unable to articulate what I really needed.

I distinctly remember a significant season in our daughter's life when our whole family was deeply impacted by her emotional trauma, and we as a family were carrying that stress.

On some occasions, people in our local circles attempted to reassure me with the declaration "I am praying for you!" Although I very much appreciated the prayers, there were many times when I actually needed tangible, practical, and physical help from them. I too was praying and faithfully leaning into my faith, only to discover that some people I thought might be the answer to my prayers were either unable or unwilling to involve themselves.

A few times friends asked us what we needed. My answer was often "I don't know." Sometimes I might have been overwhelmed and really not have known what I needed. At other times, I did know what I needed but was just too numb or overwhelmed to make one more decision.

Then one day, an out-of-state friend texted me and said announced, "I'm sending a meal. I am ordering it online from a local restaurant near you and having it delivered." Voila! Ah—relief and breathing room. She knew that I needed help during the afterschool and supper hours to offset the stress that was building up around our daughter's narrative. Besides that, she knew I was dealing with primary and secondary PTSD (post-traumatic stress disorder) that I carried from a previous traumatic event. This individual was not only a good friend but a young mother with small children at home (minus the challenges of adoption), and she simply wanted to help a fellow mother. She met a need of mine with one with which she was familiar in the parenting world. This small yet significant solution made a tremendous impact on me in a very challenging season for our family.

As things got more complicated in our story, I could see new people coming into our support circle. This gave me hope that we were not going to be left alone and forgotten in our struggles. I could feel my sense of hope increasing as well. I was realizing that I didn't feel as alone and numb as I had before, because I knew that there were friends who were willing to help in tangible and practical ways. I kept a list of those names in case I would need to reach out in the future.

Since we were a family in crisis, without knowing ahead of time the duration of it, we decided to take things week by week in terms of what was needed in our home. However, for our daughter and for me personally, it was going to be a day-to-day adjustment. I was learning that not all needs were as urgent as they felt.

We also uncovered some major needs in our marriage. My husband is an amazing guy with a great heart. In this season of increasing challenges, he worked hard to provide for our family and take care of us financially. He was carrying added stress around the growing mountain of medical bills that we were accumulating, from medications to counseling to unexpected hospitalizations.

However, he is also an introvert who isn't a fan of emotional stress. Who is? I am not, either, but it doesn't usually wear me out as much as it did him. He is a man with many strengths, one of which is his ability (and desire) to stay on top of the many physical tasks that exist in the home. He is a huge fan of "getting things done because they need to get done." Consequently, he dealt with the emotional stress in the home by accomplishing tasks. I wish I had understood that better when our kids were little, but I didn't. I interpreted his introverted, task-driven behaviors as rejection of me. That wasn't the case at all, he would often assure me. He simply needed to tackle a task because it would have a start and an end; that in itself would give him a strong sense of satisfaction and accomplishment. Emotional and relational stress were exhausting to him because it felt as though they were never-ending.

Then there is me. I am a highly relational extrovert. When there is any kind of stress (or even the absence of it), I want to write, talk, and share about it. I need to vent, to be heard and listened to. I need to experience a relational level of care for me. I also understand that my needs appear to grow exponentially when hormones, lack of food, or lack of sleep are contributing factors.

The question then becomes "How do I get my relational needs met from a husband who leans toward tasks, and how does he get his needs met from a wife who is clearly needing much more relational interaction than he might be able to give?" I realized that my husband was not designed to meet all my needs. And I was not designed to meet all his needs. We need a circle of relationships outside our marriage to supplement and support it.

Below is my attempt—with my husband's input—to provide you with some suggestions for getting your individual, marital, and family needs met. They have worked for us, but keep in mind that they are suggestions. They are not gender specific and don't always address specific individual needs. And remember that tasks will always be available to do, while relationships and people may not be as available or as accessible as you would like.

Suggestions for having your individual, marital, and family needs met:

1. Make a list of friends who can support you in tangible ways.

2. Keep the facts the facts. Be clear about physical, emotional, and spiritual needs.

3. Don't get upset when someone serves you from their place of wiring.

4. Seek to understand rather than to be understood.

5. Reach out to friends and affirm their efforts. They aren't walking in your shoes and don't always know or understand the impact of their efforts in your time of need.

6. Remember that not all your emotional needs can and will be met—or should be met—by your spouse or partner.

7. Be deliberate and intentional about doing the basics (e.g., taking a shower).

8. Get a handle on what your needs are, and don't be ashamed to state them out loud. When my husband finally asked what I needed, I was surprised by my own response. My expressed needs had nothing to do with the physical but everything to do with the emotional and relational.

9. Tackling and completing tasks is restorative to a task-oriented person. Relational time is restorative to a relational person.

10. When you understand that you are having a difficult time meeting the needs of your spouse or partner, keep the lines of communication open. If your relationship isn't united and healthy, the challenges from parenting a child with trauma could be detrimental to your marriage.

11. Much effort is needed from both sides of the marriage. Being gracious regarding each other's approach in the midst of it all is crucial in order for peace to inhabit the relationship.

Want to help a family in need?

1. Look at your resources (spiritual, emotional, mental, financial, physical, etc.) and see how you might share them with a family who has adopted or is caring for a challenging child. Oftentimes, what "looks" like a small thing may make a big impact.

2. Take the initiative to do something simple, like providing a meal or giving a gift card for take-out food. That may open the door for more dialogue about what the person/family really needs.

3. Understand that the behaviors you see in others' children might not be consistent with how that behave at home. Or perhaps the behaviors are worse when that child is in public. The two worlds coexist.

4. Learn to *accept* the family and their needs rather than just *tolerating* them.

5. Do you believe in prayer? "Adopt" a family and pray for them weekly; let them know you are doing that; this awareness will give them strength and hope and let them know that God sees and hears and is providing for them.

6. Send encouraging notes from time to time. Many of us deal with so much negativity during our parenting journey that we have the potential to lose sight of our positive qualities as parents.

7. Don't offer opinions, especially if you have no experience with parenting a child—let alone one grappling with trauma, triggers, and relinquishment pain.

8. Listen. The ability to listen well requires you to be silent. You might have noticed that *listen* and *silent* share the same letters.

9. When or where you are able, go to their home and take time to engage with the child who has challenges so the parent can do something else uninterrupted (such as spending quality time with the other children or some alone time with their spouse or partner).

10. Help by volunteering to clean their home occasionally, or even a few times a month.

11. Initiate a *scheduled* night out with girl or guy friends, or a couples' date night. This gives the parent(s) something positive to look forward to.

12. Help with grocery shopping, make some meals for the freezer, or help the family with laundry or yard work.

13. Attend an appointment with the parent to help with smaller children.

14. Read a book on therapeutic methods to better enable you to help with the child(ren).

15. Ask "What can I do to help?" Then wait for an answer and leave with an action plan. This shows the parent that you

"see" them and that there really is a village around them for support.

16. Engage the other children in the home in fun activities so they don't get lost amid the challenging dynamics.

17. Come and hang out at the house so the parent can take a nap or hot bath (this can be a *huge* help for a single parent).

18. Wash the car or do small fix-it projects around the house.

19. Become a big sister or big brother to the children in an adoptive family.

20. Provide or sponsor music lessons, art lessons, tutoring, or help with homework.

21. If you are able, help financially with gift cards for activities or gas.

HOW ABOUT YOU?

What is it you need?

Who is it you need?

In what ways do you feel seen and heard (validated)?

Ask "How can I help?" to a family in your community.

23

You Signed Up for This

At the start of 2017 there were deep and challenging thoughts brewing in my heart. More than usual. We were in the thick of a variety of situations that were challenging our personal and spiritual values and consuming our time and emotions, and we had a lot of questions . . . with very few answers. In a few different conversations, we were met with some variation of the reminder "You signed up for this." This was usually not the statement I wanted or needed at that moment.

In some cases, the speaker was specifically referring to our choice to adopt, while in others the comment was directed at our choosing parenthood in general. In our case, this statement carried more weight in light of our adoption journey. Whether or not you are a parent, I implore you to consider how you might come alongside a parent or family with biological children or children who have arrived through foster care or of adoption. The need for a caring and authentic support system is real.

Many of us who have adopted children have experienced deep love and courage we didn't think we were capable of, while learning to navigate those sometimes treacherous and challenging waters. When we look back, we can clearly see our successes and our failures. My attention was often on my failures or shortfalls. The struggle was real. This book is a product of all those successes and failures, perceived or real. The thoughts that were brewing in my heart eventually found their way into my journal and now into print for you to be reminded that you are not alone with your struggle.

As I wrote this book, I had to be honest with myself. I also needed to find the strength to face my failures and realistically view and assess my successes. And I wanted the truth of our journey to be an encouragement and a catalyst for hope for you, the reader.

There are many unforeseen challenges in the adoption journey—areas in which the prospective parents "don't know what they don't know" before the fact—and I now recognize the many things I *did not* know I had signed up for. Among them, in our situation:

- Consistent rejection.

- Behavioral issues that were damaging to our daughter and deeply impactful to the other children in the home.

- Thousands of dollars and countless hours of appointments with counselors, agencies, mental health clinicians, medical experts, etc.

- Loss of friends and family because of our choice to parent "someone else's kid" (as some have termed adoption and personally expressed to us).

- Isolation that led to deep loneliness.

- A marriage that would be tested to its limits.

- Fractured relationships at times with our biological children.

- Caring more for our daughter than she did for herself.

- Questioning my calling and role as a mother.

- Judgmental or critical comments of judgment from those who should have known better.

What I *did* sign up for included:

- Loving in the best way I knew.

- Sharing "my" space with a girl. (Most moms will understand this—lol!)

- Learning every step of the way.

- Living in Truth: hers, mine, and the Bible's.

- Trusting God to write the story.

- Praying faithfully for all our children.

- Being committed, as best I could to the needs of all our children.

- Helping our daughter realize her potential.

- Working and growing toward being part of the solution, as opposed to exacerbating or perpetuating problems.

- Growing a girl into a woman.

- Surrounding myself with fellow truth-tellers.

Just because we answered the call to adopt didn't mean that we knew what was waiting for us on the road ahead. One day, when I didn't know what else to do, I listened to a small, still voice in my heart whispering, "Good, now you are ready to fully realize what I called you to!" Our parenting road was paved with great joy, sorrow, weariness, feeling overwhelmed, discouragement, excitement, anticipation of both positive and negative outcomes, a deep peace, chaotic experiences, confusion, a deep and inexpressible love in my heart for our daughter and our sons, deep convictions that were challenged, a freedom *to be* and a sense of suppressed freedom—sometimes simultaneously, rejection, unresolved pain, perseverance, resilience, endurance, and the list (a jumble of positive, negative, and sometimes neutral) goes on . . .

I knew that, if I leaned into my faith, I would be okay, and this gave me the hope that our family would be, too.

As I grew to accept and come to terms with what I had and had not "signed up for," I grew stronger, bolder, more focused, and more determined to make our relationship work and to heal, enabling me to pray for the same for our daughter and our sons.

Signing documents to finalize the adoption was met with excitement and relief. But the unknowns of the road ahead eventually taught us what our family was made of. At the time we didn't know what the road of adoption would look like. But we did know that we were committed to our daughter and to our whole family and that we would do whatever it took to survive and learn to thrive.

HOW ABOUT YOU?

Can you relate to our adoption journey? How would you articulate yours?

What has "heart work" looked like in your story?

Who in your story is supporting you unconditionally through the ups-and-downs? (Maybe today presents another opportunity to say, "Thank you for being on my team.")

How are you choosing to walk this path of parenting?

What *did* you sign up for?

Victorianna's Message

A personal and heartfelt message we received from our daughter a year after she was reunited with her birth mother:

Forgiveness is a key to a lot. I mean I've really thought back to stuff you used to say, Mrs. Kinita, and I've come to some realization that you knew what you were talking about and everything good you and Mr. Ken provided in my life I greatly appreciated it. I mean then I didn't really know how to show it. I just thought it was supposed to be me and myself in the world, but I've learned to let people in.

Love, Victorianna

About Kinita

Kinita has lived cross-culturally for almost five decades between India, Canada, and the USA. She has obtained decades of experience serving diverse communities in a variety of roles as she and her husband Ken, of almost 30 years, were raising their three biological sons and adopted daugher.

Her treasured professional accomplishments are that of being a publishied author, international speaker, and cultural coach. In between writing, coaching, and hosting workshops, she records coaching videos and interviews guests for her podcast *Growing Forward Together*. In her free time, she loves spending time with her husband as they relish their empty nest years, serving in a variety of volunteer positions, traveling, and enjoying deep conversations with friends over coffee or a meal.

Kinita is passionate about learning, teaching, growing stronger connections with people, and helping others live into their best self.

Made in the USA
Monee, IL
25 February 2022